THE RISE AND FALL OF THE POSTER

MAURICE RICKARDS

DAVID AND CHARLES

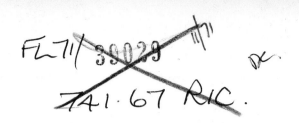
Designed by Maurice Rickards

First published 1971

ISBN 0 7153 5315 2

Set by Alden and Mowbray Limited Oxford
and printed by Latimer Trend and Company Whitstable

Allner, Walter H., 151
Anquetin, L., 46
Atherton, John, 131
Bacon, C. W., 127
Batty, Dora, 97
Beardsley, Aubrey, 36
Beggarstaff Brothers, 44
Bernard, Francis, 128
Boccasile, Gino, 136, 137
Bompard, Luigi, 23
Bonini, Ezio, 158
Borgoni, Mario, 63
Bradley, William, 37, 52
Brangwyn, Sir Frank, 90
Brown, Gregory, 72
Brun, Donald, 149

Calabresi, Aldo, 158
Cappiello, Leonetto, 67, 71, 121
Carlu, Jean, 109, 132
Caspel, J. G. van, 48
Cassandre, A. M., 98, 100, 118, 125
Caxton, William, 1
Chéret, Jules, 27
Choubrac, Alfred, 50
Chmielewski, Witold, 145
Christy, Howard Chandler, 57, 58
Codognato, Plinio, 93
Cooper, Austin, 103, 129
Cremonesi, Carmelo, 165

Dearing, Richard, 164
Dorda, E., 42
Dudovich, Marcello, 96, 116

Eber, Elk, 126
Eckersley, Tom, 156
Edelmann, Heinz, 170, 175
Erdt, Hans Rudi, 51

Erhardt, Georg, 158
Fancher, Louis, 53
Fischer, Otto, 39
Flagg, James Montgomery, 59
Flowers, Adrian, 164
Fouqueray, Charles, 89
Freedman, Barnett, 107
Frei, Arthur, 166

Games, Abram, 134, 143
Gardner, F., 83
Giacometti, Augusto, 104
Gotha, Fritz Koch, 76
Grieder, Heiner, 166

Hassáll, John, 73
Hayman, Bob, 161
Henry, Max, 163
Hohenstein, Adolfo, 28, 45
Hohlwein, Ludwig, 62, 69, 122, 133

Ivanov, Viktor, 139

Kauffer, E. McKnight, 119, 120
Keimel, Hermann, 114
Keller, Ernst, 106
Kollwitz, Käte, 80
Krol, Stan, 154

Leete, Alfred, 61
Leupin, Herbert, 146
Little, William, 144
Lunel, F., 31

Martin, Ed de, 161
Matter, Herbert, 112
Meidinger, Gérard, 142
Metlicovitz, Leopoldo, 41, 77
Millais, Sir John, 24
Moor, D. S.
    (Dimitri Stakheyevitch Orlov), 94

Mucha, Alfons, 34, 40
Munari, Bruno, 152
Newbould, Frank, 75
Nicholson, William, 44
Nizzoli, Marcello, 101, 115
Paléologue, Jean, 30
Petzold, Willy, 124
Picasso, Pablo, 148
Pintori, Giovanni, 147
Pryde, James, 44
Purvis, Tom, 81, 91, 102
'Rae', 66
Rickards, Maurice, 141
Rosen, Hans, 87

Sanders, C. Cavania, 110
Santambrogio, —, 88
Savignac, Raymond, 155, 159
Scott, Septimus E., 79
'Sem', 60
Smale, B. H., 43
Smith, Ray, 174
Steinlen, Théophile, 32, 35, 38, 49
Stiller, Alfred, 95

Taylor, Horace, 99
Terzi, Aleardo, 54
Throop, George Enos, 92
Toulouse-Lautrec, Henri de, 26
Trepkowski, Tadeusz, 150

Ungerer, Tomi, 162

Vallotton, F., 25
Venna, Lucio, 82
Villa, Aleardo, 29
Vincent, René, 85

Walker, Frederick, 21
Wiertz, Jupp, 70

Among the many organizations and individuals who have helped in the preparation of this book the author and publishers would like especially to thank the following: Association d'Enterprises d'Affichage; Bodleian Library; Bovril Ltd; St Bride Foundation Printing Library; British Museum; British Petroleum Ltd; British Poster Advertising Association; Christian Aid; Collezione Bertarelli; Collet, Dickenson, Pearce & Partners Ltd; Alfred H. Cooper & Sons Ltd; Alfred Dunhill Ltd; Tom Eckersley; Edizioni La Pietra; Evening News Ltd; Abram Games; G & B Arts Ltd; Gibbs Proprietaries Ltd (Pears); Habitat Ltd; Johanna Harrison; Imperial War Museum; Instituto Cubano de Amistad con los Pueblos; John Johnson Collection; Johnson Riddle Ltd; Stan Krol; Yolanda Martelli; Marx Memorial Library; Norman Messenger; Mills & Allen Ltd; National Bus Company; The Poster Shops Ltd; Prunier's Restaurant, London; Shell Mex-BP Ltd; Skegness Urban District Council; Texaco Ltd; Union des Villes et Communes belges; Universal Pictures Ltd; Victoria and Albert Museum; Dino Villani; Waterlow & Sons Ltd.

THE RISE AND FALL OF THE POSTER

Broadsheet and Proclamation

HISTORICALLY SPEAKING, THE POSTER is a new invention. Its beginnings—and, as will be seen, its endings—are bound up with the evolution of the major visual technologies. It is with the advent of printing, earliest of the techniques of multiple production, that we must identify the poster's origins.

To go back, as some have done, into the mists of time, to the trade signs on the walls at Pompeii, to Egyptian hieroglyphics and even to the cave paintings of Altamira, is to take too long and academic a run at it altogether. The poster, at once a product and an instrument of the consumer society, is a child of our own time; it begins not with the Trajan column but with Gutenberg, Caxton and the rest.

Before the advent of printing, though the poster may have been a gleam in man's eye, it remained a gleam unrealised. The concept—of an item multiply produced, a separate item fixed to a wall for public view—required the development of the technique of graphic reproduction. By definition (it may be said without unduly begging the question) the poster is a *reproduction*.

The matter has been expressed elsewhere: 'The twentieth-century connoisseur lays down clear-cut rules as to what is and what is not a poster. Firstly, says the connoisseur, the poster is a separate sheet, *affixed* to an existing surface (as opposed to those markings and images rendered directly on the surface). Secondly, it must embody a *message*; a mere decorative image is not enough. Thirdly, it must be *publicly displayed*. Finally, it must have been multiply produced; a single hand-done notice is not a poster within the meaning of the Act . . .'*

Though in some respects arbitrary, this definition has the merit of cutting out much that might otherwise confuse us. By this standard, clearly, a slogan daubed on a wall is not a poster. Nor is a hand-written notice saying 'Back in ten minutes'. Nor are the

* *'Posters of Protest and Revolution', Adams and Dart, 1970*

words on the Trajan column, the Pompeii murals, the tablets brought down from the mountain by Moses, or Van Gogh's sunflowers.

In one respect at least—in the matter of the poster's separateness from the surface it goes on—etymology is on our side: a poster is, plainly, something 'posted up'. The English word, said to derive from the use of street boundary posts as display sites in the seventeenth century, offers moral support, but the French and German words, *affiche* and *anschlag*, with their unmistakable overtones of 'sticking on' or '— up', settle the matter finally.

With the poster's fourfold characteristics settled once and for all, the connoisseur pauses. As with all definitions, there is a penumbra of uncertainty: it must be conceded that certain items—printed notices, instruction charts and the like—which, for all that they may meet the prescribed requirements, still fail to qualify as posters. For the filtration of this last residue, the connoisseur resorts to the final refuge of the expert: 'If I say it is a poster, it is a poster. Otherwise, clearly, it is not a poster.'

Some writers have sought to clarify the point. Susan Sontag, in her introduction to Stermer's *Art of Revolution*, draws a sharp dividing line through the penumbra. 'Posters are not simply public notices,' she says; '. . . the poster, as distinct from the public notice, presupposes the modern concept of the public—in which the members of a society are defined primarily as spectators and consumers. A public notice aims to inform or command. A poster aims to seduce, to exhort, to sell, to educate, to convince, to appeal. Whereas a public notice distributes information to interested or alert citizens, a poster reaches out to grab those who might otherwise pass it by . . .'

There is much in what Miss Sontag says. But it is also true that many a so-called public notice seeks 'to seduce, to exhort, to sell' etc. Is the announcement of Mr Brayshaw [20],* with its blend of seduction, exhortation, and sales appeal, a poster or a notice? Is the London-to-Salisbury post-chaise announcement [8] a poster, or a notice, or an announcement? And what of the blandishments of Messrs Varnet & Company of Lyons [2], and Messrs Woolley & Dix of Denmark Street across the page [7]? It will be seen that, by any standards, the area of uncertainty is broader than at first appears.

In all ordinary reckonings of poster chronology, when all the more obvious non-starters have been eliminated, Martin Luther and William Caxton jostle for first place. Luther, with his ninety-five points of dissent on a large poster nailed to the door of Wittenberg Castle church in 1517, comes close. But he must be disqualified, not only on account of his date, which is forty years later than Caxton, but also because his was a hand-done, one-off affair. As we have seen, by present definition, the Luther poster was not a poster.

We may also wonder whether the Caxton one was. Though undeniably a printed reproduction, it was so small (barely larger than a playing-card) that it might have passed for a leaflet rather than a poster [1]. As an advertisement, not only in size but in editorial tone, it certainly must rank as one of the most modest of all time. Its claim to posterhood lies solely in the implications of its foot-line; *Supplico stet cedula* 'Please

---

* *Numerals in brackets refer to illustrations*

leave this paper in place'—presumably on a wall.

It is significant that it was Caxton who saw the value of the multiply reproduced announcement; he was, after all, in the business of multiple reproduction. But it is also significant that centuries were to pass before the concept of the printed poster fully emerged. Apart from books, there were few other commodities whose scale of production could claim a mass market. For its full development, in both form and content, the poster was to await the coming of an industrialised society.

In the meantime, however, there were specific fields in which a mass audience was essential. One was government. Another was recruitment. Another was entertainment. Another—rebellion and insurrection. There was also the buying and selling of property —real estate, livestock and slaves. There was also the opening up of transport services, packhorse carriers, the waggoners and the stage- and mail-coaches. It was in these fields that the printed poster slowly developed. It was here that the area of uncertainty, the shading off from notice to announcement and from announcement to poster, broadened.

In a less literate and sophisticated society the printed word had an authority of its own. The mere presence of a proclamation, pasted on a barn door or nailed to a tree, was an item of interest in itself. To the average citizen the distinction between an official announcement and a commercially inspired broadsheet was blurred; whatever it was, it was new, important and commanding. It was also a direct point of contact between 'them'—the authorities—and 'us', the ordinary people; as such it was something of a privilege to behold.

The official proclamation, with its stark black lettering and its inevitable signature or coat-of-arms, developed an idiom of its own. Verbose, self-righteous and self-justified, it was a universal instrument of rule. It declared war, raised the price of bread, threatened to shoot hostages, exaggerated victories, justified retreats, ordered rejoicings, stamped out mutinies and deeply mourned dead rulers while simultaneously welcoming their replacements. For the most part, such was the illiteracy of its readership, it had to be read out loud by the man who posted it up.

The history of Europe may be read in proclamations. There were proclamations, too, not only from the invading enemy but from dissident cells and factions. The idiom was adopted by the under-dogs who, in counter-proclamations, spoke back to authority in terms of authority. For long periods the printed proclamation was the sole medium of mass communication. In museums and libraries all over Europe they still remain, proclaiming to each other for posterity.

Initially, proclamations consisted only of wording, but slowly they acquired pictorial airs and graces. It became fashionable, with the use of wood engraving, to mitigate the starkness of the written word with images. The imperious recruiting bill, once uncompromising in its typographic call, now blandished with seductive artwork [2, 9, 10]. The area of confusion became broader still; was this an order, a request, or an invitation? Here was this circus picture [3], with the gentleman leaping over four horses at once: an order, a request, or an invitation? A poster, a proclamation or an announcement?

The pictorial wood engraving, starting life as a mere decoration, was to become a major ingredient. Standard blocks—engravings of general subjects which could be used repeatedly—became part of the printer's stock-in-trade. The mail-coach announcement, whether it was for the run between Manchester and Edinburgh or London and Brighton, carried the same thunderous coach and four. (Later, in London in the eighteenth century, the same principle was applied to printed reports of executions at Tyburn and Newgate. A set-piece drawing of a scaffold, complete with crowd and hangman, had a scaffold-space for as many prisoners as occasion demanded. Separate hanging figures were inserted into the block to the number required. The completed block appeared as a title piece to the news story.)

Widespread as the use of wood engraving finally became, its progress was slow. For the most part the poster (proclamation, notice, announcement, or whatever it was) stood by its lettering alone. Working with nothing more ambitious than their well-worn stocks of wooden lettering, rules and borders, printers nevertheless managed a fair degree of variety. Some brought the disposition of words on a sheet of paper to a fine art. In the generality, what they lacked in aesthetic resources they made up for in enthusiasm and ingenuity. Often it seemed that the very limitations they worked under imposed a special unity and integrity on the result. The United States election poster of 1864 [6], typical of the genre as it developed in the nineteenth century, has an exuberance inherent in the medium. The lavish multiplicity of type faces, the jam-packed overcrowding, the condensed and rough-cut lettering combine to produce not only a sense of excitement but of structural unity. George F. Nesbitt, who printed (and presumably designed) the work, was a natural master of his craft.

In distinctly more sober vein, a proclamation from the Palace at Vienna [13], reflects its own urgencies and its own visual unity. Here the classic 'black letter' of Germany, a medieval survival into the nineteenth—and even the twentieth—century, speaks with dignity and a passable show of decision. No one would guess from its air of authority that His Imperial Majesty, feeble-minded and ailing, had been ignominiously packed off to Switzerland to escape the mob. (He finally abdicated in December of the same year; 1848 was a bad year for majesty and proclamations.)

Official printed announcements are often less confident than they seem. Sometimes they are more confident than the situation warrants. The decree of Napoleon III, published in Boulogne in 1840 [19], over-reached itself by a very long way. Printed some weeks in advance in London, where his prospective excellency Louis-Napoleon had been biding his time for a *coup d'état*, it was taken over as part of his invasion equipment for nailing up in suitable places on arrival. It will be noticed that the precise date was left blank to allow for the exigencies of the occasion. With a tricolour, a band of some sixty supporters in a variety of *ad hoc* uniforms, a stock of printed 'decrees' and little else, the party sailed openly to Boulogne on the Gravesend boat. Perhaps not surprisingly, the mission failed. The invader was imprisoned. Eight years were to pass before he tried again, this time by more orthodox means, and (surprisingly) succeeded.

Throughout his career he showed great faith in the printed decree; like many decree-makers, he came to view the existence of the printed sheet almost as accomplishment of the effect it sought to achieve. Though operating in an inverse sense, it appears to have embodied the principle of sticking pins in the image of an adversary.

'What shall the doctor prescribe if the state is ill?' asked one writer, 'Why, a decree! and then if that is not enough, another and another . . .' Among the most frequently occurring engravings in the illustrated journals of the period is a view of citizens gathered round the figure of a billposter as he slaps up a new decree across the remnants of its predecessors. It is clear that, as he nailed up the 1840 decree in Boulogne, Louis-Napoleon expected the Bourbons to have toppled by the last nail.

The London/Boulogne item is by no means alone in having been printed, so to speak, abroad. A more recent specimen, printed in English and German, and also prepared some time in advance, is directed to the people of Germany. It was posted up early in 1945 and it begins 'I, Dwight D. Eisenhower, Supreme Commander, Allied Expeditionary Force, do hereby proclaim as follows . . .'

In the clutter of European history the two-language proclamation is by no means rare. In the eighteenth and nineteenth centuries, with the incessant grouping and re-grouping of blocs and alliances, bilingualism crept in everywhere. Here, unlike the Eisenhower example, in which English preceded German down the page, the requirement was normally for parity. The admonition to the citizens of Strasbourg [17] is a typically tactful side-by-side example. In cases where three or more languages were involved the tendency was, of course, for wider and wider proclamations; it must be concluded that precedence from left to right is less invidious than from top to bottom.

'Bill-stickers Will be Prosecuted'

If the poster has its origins in the proclamation, it partakes in some measure of its special magic—the power of the printed word. Since its inception, printing has been seen, not only by the ignorant but by the educated minority, as very powerful magic indeed. No sooner had the invention gained currency than it ran into trouble with Authority. Like the Duke of Wellington, who saw the advent of the railways as a dangerous means whereby the labouring classes could make contact with each other, fifteenth- and sixteenth-century Authority saw printing as a threat to dogma.

Those who had initially encouraged it with patronage, when they saw what they had espoused, underwent a sudden change of heart. Here, unless it was kept strictly under control, was a social force of virtually boundless implication. By 1500 it was running away with itself. Pope Alexander issued a bull against the unlicensed printing of books; in France, every printer risked being taken for a heretic. One of them, Etienne Dolet, was in fact tortured and burnt at the stake.

In England, too, Authority clamped down. Caxton's successors, hitherto free to print what they liked, came under the ordinances of the Stationers' Company. In 1586 it was laid down that all printing be confined to the universities of Oxford and Cambridge and the City of London. Later, in 1637, typefounding was pronounced to be a separate industry and was separately controlled.

The freedom of the press, corollary of freedom of speech, is a concept of uneasy acceptance. Throughout history, by every authority, printing has been viewed with something less than enthusiasm. In Britain, the tax on newspapers, avowedly a revenue-raising device (but universally recognised as a form of censorship), was finally removed only in the 1850s. Under the British colonial rule in America, the tax on newspapers was a major cause of discontent; it may be said to have helped to spark the powder-keg. Certainly it was the printed word, in the form of many scores of books, pamphlets and broadsheets, that gave form to the drive to independence. Authority was right: printing was the most powerful force since the invention of gunpowder.

The poster, itself no more than a posted printed page, also came under fire. *Bill-stickers will be prosecuted* is more than a threat; it has the makings of an eternal truth.

In France, in 1534, a diarist records that town criers had been ordered by the court to announce the offer of a reward to anyone divulging the names of illicit billstickers; any citizen knowing of such a person and failing to inform the authorities, or keeping such persons in hiding, would be 'publicly burnt in the town'. At the same time, Authority staked its own claim to poster rights. In 1539 Francis I proclaimed on the subject of proclamations: 'We desire that these present commands be published in each month of the year at every crossroad of this town of Paris and of the outskirts of the same, to the sound of trumpets and by public crier. Moreover that they be fixed to a board written on parchment in large letters in all the sixteen districts of the said city of Paris and said outskirts in the most visible and commanding places therein so that they may be known and heard by one and all. And it shall be unlawful to remove the said boards under pain of corporal punishment . . .'

An edict from Paris in 1652 threatened the billsticker with flogging. In the following year a further decree forbade the printing of placards without the authority of the king; the penalty was death. Decrees of one sort or another (themselves multiply posted) followed frequently. In 1721, in a final attempt to stem the tide, the government issued a decree regulating the (now recognised) *Corporation des Colleurs*, or Society of Bill-stickers, and limiting the number of practitioners in the City of Paris to forty. Even then it was required that a copy of each poster be deposited in advance in the King's Library.

The widespread restraints imposed upon printing were a severe brake on its development. What had started in the middle 1400s as a commanding new technology now fell into something not far short of disrepute. In some areas it was virtually abandoned. In Britain, the Star Chamber decree of 1367 resulted in the transfer of the typefounding industry to Holland. For the British printer this meant that he was cut off from one of the prime materials of his craft—type itself. It was not until 1695 that he was free again.

In the meantime, in London and a number of other European cities, there had begun to emerge a graphic form which served in some measure as a substitute, and which had its own place in the unfolding history of the poster.

Tradesman's Card to Colour Poster

The 'tradesman's card', or 'shopkeeper's bill' as it was sometimes called, had evolved almost by accident. Its origins are hazy and there has always been doubt as to its primary purpose. Ambrose Heal, writing in 1925, says, 'The exact purpose of the trade card is not generally agreed upon. Some say that it was primarily as an account, and that it was frequently used for this purpose cannot be denied . . . But when these [accounts] occur on the face, it is only where the blank space provides opportunity . . . More usually . . . the engraving giving the trader's name, his sign and his address, and the setting forth of the list of his wares, occupies the whole of the face of the Bill . . . This announcement . . . of his shop is the first and principal use of the tradesman's card . . .'

From the examples that survive (many of them, as Heal says, bearing invoice jottings and other notes) it is clear that they were an item of universal application. The card advertising Mr Thomas Edwards, supplier of asses' milk [11], is typical. They were small enough to be used as *aides-mémoire* for new customers, large enough to carry notes and instructions to messengers and to be used as giveaway leaflets to passers-by. They were an all-purpose seventeenth-century compliments-slip-cum-promotion-piece. There can be little doubt that the 'cards' (most of which were, in fact, printed on thin paper) were also used as leaflets for slipping under potential customers' front doors and for pasting up on walls and fences. In this last capacity they may be considered as a direct link in the genealogy of the poster.

The London tradesman's card came into general use in the early 1700s. In its earliest form it is little more than a representation of a tradesman's signboard—a feature which, in the absence of any system of street addresses, was a vital adjunct to the business of the eighteenth-century shopkeeper. All over Europe, in an illiterate and addressless society, the signboard had become so universal as to be a nuisance. Headroom in the narrow streets and alleys of the cities lessened year by year. The creaking of the signs as they swayed in the wind, and the continual danger of their falling on passers-by, eventually led to their formal abolition.

In London, the symbols used on the signs were carried over to the tradesmen's cards and remained in use for years after the signboards had come down. Later the card carried decorative ornament to offset the starkness of the signboard sketch, and later still it bore illustrations of wares and services for sale. Finally the signboard motif disappeared, leaving a decorative presentation of the tradesman's sales story. With the introduction of street numbering, directions for finding the premises became less picturesque. But the habit of descriptive indications died hard; the asses' milk item,

dated 1781, was some twenty years behind the times.

The tradesman's card, initially a crude expedient, soon developed an idiom and an elegance of its own. Moving out of the woodcut stage, it began to attract the attention of the engraver, who brought to it a refinement almost beyond its function.

Until this time the field of the public announcement had been dominated by relief printing, in which the inked impression was conveyed to paper from a raised surface. Wood, carved by hand in the form of pictures or movable type, or metal type cast in a foundry, was inked with a roller and pressed to the surface of the paper. The technique of the engraver, however, uses the sunken parts of the plate as the printing area. After inscribing the surface of the metal plate with a fine tool, the artist then inks the whole surface of the plate, filling the incisions with ink; then, with the surface of the plate wiped clean and the incisions alone retaining ink, the plate is pressed into contact with the printing paper. This method, slower but much finer in effect than relief printing, had been the medium of fine artists since the middle of the fifteenth century—among them, pre-eminently, Albrecht Dürer. In the London of the 1700s it was applied, among other things, to the shopkeeper's trade card.

The convention flourished into a distinctive art-form. By 1720 one William Hogarth (twenty-three years of age, and recently set up on his own) had designed his own card: *William Hogarth, Engraver*. Within a few years he had done designs for some two dozen other persons—among them a boxer, a fan-maker, two tobacconists and an upholsterer. If any one of his customers succumbed to the temptation of pasting up his card in public, Hogarth must qualify as the first among a distinguished list of artists whose work has appeared in poster form.

Although perfectly suited to small-scale use, the art of the engraver cannot be said to offer more than a passing contribution to the poster proper. For the larger effect, for the attention-grabbing stridency of the public announcement, the delicacies of the engraving are inappropriate.

In the matter of lettering it was a mere mimic; laboriously it parodied the conventions of typography, imitating the style of movable type—without succeeding. As relief printing gained efficiency and impact, the engraved letter took refuge even more tenaciously in 'copperplate' curlicues and scrollwork. In the family tree of the poster the trade card was a line without issue.

In the meantime, striving for the bolder effects of the true poster, the woodcut image pushed ahead. Hand-cut wooden lettering became fatter, bolder and more commanding. Metal type, too, which until the 1800s had been dominated by the relative lightness and airiness of book production, fattened up spectacularly. In both wood and metal the spindly letter forms seen in the 1770s' post-chaise announcement [8] gave way to the exuberance of new 'fat' types by Thorne, Thorowgood, and their successors [14]. From the point of view of lettering at least, the idiom of the poster was in process of emerging.

But still there was no mechanical means of producing the printing block. As it had done for centuries past, this still relied on the individual skill of the human hand. It could not readily be enlarged or reduced at will, and—what was the biggest limiting factor—it was confined to the solid printing areas of the ordinary woodcut. The image it produced was either 'all-ink' or 'no-ink'. Except by stipple and cross-hatching, the tones and gradations between these two extremes were unattainable. Printed almost invariably in one colour—black—and produced on machines that had changed little from Caxton's time, the pictorial poster was slow to emerge.

Not until 1871, when Frederick Walker's design for *The Woman in White* appeared [21] did the woodcut finally take over from the wording, and the verve and impact of its execution stand up on its own. Walker's view of the poster as a medium was far-sighted: 'I am impressed on doing all I can,' he wrote of this, his only excursion into the medium, 'with a first attempt at what I consider might develop into a most important branch of design.' When it had been completed, engraved on wood by William Hooper and posted all over London for the opening of the play at the Olympic Theatre, the design was a minor sensation. In its boldness and simplicity, its arresting sense of dramatic action, and above all in its visual economy, it may be described as one of the first true posters. Walker, Royal Academician, illustrator, painter in oils and watercolours, was popular in his day as an academic artist, but *The Woman in White* design shows signs of living longer than any of the rest of his work.

The Woman in White was the beginning of a new era in the history of the poster, but in another sense it was also the end of an era. The development of relief printing in 'half-tones' (as opposed to the solid blacks and whites of the woodcut) was slow. It had always been realised that the illusion of tonal gradation depended on the relative density of 'granulation' of the image. Black dots tightly packed in a small area look blacker than the same dots spread over a bigger area. In relief printing, the problem was to remain unsolved until the development, at about the turn of the century, of photographic techniques and the 'half-tone' process. Only then did the half-tone dot (still in the 1970s the basic principle of half-tone picture reproduction) make possible gradations from one shade to another.

But in another process altogether—a method dating back to the previous century, and widely used as a fine-art medium—gradation effects have always been possible. Lithography, invented by Alois Senefelder in 1798, was destined to play a leading role in the rise of the poster. Here the granulation effect is provided by the texture of the stone on which the original drawing is made.

Unlike the 'relief' or 'recess' techniques of printing, which rely for their effect on two distinct planes or levels in the printing plate for the transfer of ink to the paper, lithography exploits the capacity of grease to repel water. An image, executed with a pencil containing grease, is drawn straight on to the surface of the stone by the artist. The stone is then moistened with water and rolled with an ink roller. The water-moistened areas of the stone reject the ink (which is greasy) and the grease-pencilled image accepts it. The drawing on the stone thus becomes impregnated with ink and can be used as a 'master' from which the image can be transferred by contact with paper.

Senefelder, actor and playwright, discovered the principle whilst searching for a cheap method of reproducing the texts of his plays. He soon realised he was on to a good thing; in the first years of the new century he patented the process. It was adopted as a medium by a number of the great artists of the day. Francisco Goya, Edgar Degas, Honoré Daumier and Paul Gauguin were among many distinguished practitioners.

The process was seen as a means of producing a modest number of reproductions from one drawing, the image on the stone being regarded not as an original but as a disposable intermediate stage. For commercial reproduction in quantity the process was not ideal. Not least of its drawbacks was the weight of the stones themselves. Measuring some four or five inches in thickness, the larger pieces had to be lifted with block and tackle. For multi-colour work, with each colour requiring its separate stone, the labour involved in a single picture was prodigious. Printing equipment, virtually unaltered since Senefelder's 'old originals', was cumbersome and inefficient.

The First Golden Age

In the early 1870s, at about the time when Frederick Walker's woodblock *The Woman in White* was taking shape, London saw the return visit of a French artist, Jules Chéret. Still an unknown, he came without ceremony. Chéret, who had started life as a printer of invitation cards and designer of jam-jar labels, had previously worked for a while in London, without success, as a designer. (Among his less notable works had been a catalogue for a Tottenham Court Road furniture company.) Now, however, as well as perfecting his knowledge of the lithographic process, he sought out some of the up-to-date equipment that had emerged from the Senefelder patents.

On his return to France he went into business. Setting up a lithographic mass-production plant in Paris, he became the world's first full-time poster artist. He developed his own techniques and exploited the improved productivity of the new machines. He reduced the number of colour runs per poster and he brought production costs down to commercially acceptable levels. If there is a single point in history when the poster may be said to have 'arrived', this was it. From this time on the poster was fully accepted as an instrument of public contact, a familiar item of the everyday scene. His country took Chéret to its heart; with him they took the poster.

Chéret's impact on the Paris of his time was enormous. In a career that was to last till the turn of the century and beyond, he produced nearly a thousand designs. Their lightness, simplicity and effervescent gaiety were a feature of outdoor Paris for decades. His technique, revolutionary after the sober black and white of the Paris placards, was a combination of line, tone and spatter—an excited fizz of colour and light. His theme, whatever the subject, was female beauty. 'In France,' he said, 'we have special dimensions for our posters. . . I prefer the largest size. . . as the height of a well-made woman is about 150 centimetres, a poster 240 centimetres in length affords ample space for the drawing of a figure full length. . .' He went on to add, however, that he avoided repetition: 'I am always on the look out for a new idea,' he said, untruthfully. His full-length females lasted him a life-time. The *Palais de Glace* example [27] appeared in 1894. Chéret was fifty-eight at the time and, as it turned out, there were still plenty more where she came from.

The Chéret phenomenon, new not only to Paris but to the world, may be said to represent the beginning of the modern colour poster. The transition from the typography of conventional announcements and theatre bills was immediate, complete, and stunning. Suddenly the word *affiche* took on a new meaning. Repetitious as his theme undoubtedly was, the Chéret idiom was such a break with the past that it could never pall. So at least it seemed, until the advent of Toulouse-Lautrec.

Henri de Toulouse-Lautrec, 'a shapeless little carpet-bag of a man', was driven to designing posters because of the difficulty he encountered in getting his work exhibited in the ordinary way. Undersized, deformed and a social oddity, Lautrec was intensely aware of the oddities and deformities of the world around him. Alexandre Hepp wrote of him: 'The odd, deformed and limping man was evident in his works. . . Many of his startling subjects had his own traits and appearance, as though he were obsessed by them. His looks had an influence on his work, and in the strangest fashion, again and again, the artist's body seemed to bear down on his personality.'

In the first of his posters, commissioned in 1891 by the director of the Moulin Rouge, a silhouetted figure in the foreground shows a well-known character of Paris night life. The figure is that of Valentin, dancing partner to La Goulue. The figure is that of Valentin but the spatulate fingers of the hands are the fingers of the artist himself.

Lautrec's preoccupation with what respectable people called the *demi-monde* served him well. Turning his back on the sugar and spice of the world of Chéret, he produced the *affiche-verité*. With a technique not far removed from the style of the Japanese (but far enough to be undeniably his own) he invested the poster with new significance. The *affiche* had become 'art'. (Even in far-away London the connoisseurs started calling posters *affiches*.) In his designs for cabarets, clubs and leg-shows, Lautrec was using the poster as a vehicle of self-expression. For all his undoubted grasp of the poster idiom— an idiom which he himself perfected—it must be said that for him the poster remained secondary to the design.

He became so famous that soon he was being asked to design posters for the sake of his fame alone. Sometimes the result was pointless, a Lautrec drawing with some added words. His poster for an American printing-ink manufacturer, commissioned solely because of his fame, is an example [26]. The drawing entitled *Au Concert*, and incidentally featuring one of Lautrec's friends, had only a passing relevance to printing ink. But its prestige value to the client was worth paying for. (Half a century later, with due reverence, the Art Institute of Chicago was to produce a further one hundred copies from the original plate.)

The Belle Époque of the 1890s—a decade of a sudden blossoming elegance—was the

First Golden Age of the poster. With Chéret, Lautrec and their confrères Steinlen, Grasset and Bonnard, the medium had appeared as though overnight, full-blown. But exhilarating as it all was, the impact of commerce was already apparent. On the crest of the wave, for better or for worse, the artist was espoused to causes unheard of. Lautrec himself, with what wisdom posterity may judge, when he had run out of nightlife, turned to whatever else offered. Among his less romantic subjects were an interior decorator's business, a confetti manufacturer of Charing Cross Road, London, and (disastrously) Simpson's bicycle chains.

As the concept of the commercial poster evolved, the problem posed itself: do fine art and poster art mix? With more or less reluctance, artists everywhere turned their hands to the hoardings. But in some quarters resistance was high.

In London in the middle 1880s there had been a celebrated crisis of conscience. On a morning in 1885 a man walked into the studio of Sir John Millais with a platemaker's proof in his hand. It was a colour lithograph of Sir John's painting of his grandson—'a singularly beautiful and winning child'—blowing soap bubbles through a pipe. The man was Thomas Barratt, manager of Pears' Soap. He proposed to Sir John that the picture be used as a soap poster.

As to precisely what happened next, history is unreliable. Most authorities agree that Sir John became apoplectic, but there is no doubt as to Barratt's success in talking him round. For succeed he did; young Willie Millais, with the addition of wording and a bar of Pears' soap, duly appeared on the hoardings [24]. It is a measure of the difference in contemporary taste between London and Paris that 'Bubbles' was an instant, overwhelming and still-remembered success. Millais never quite got over the slur on his artistic reputation.

Whatever their differences in visual taste, advertisers in both London and Paris long retained the idea of the 'picture that could be used as a poster'. As in the Ault & Wiborg case, as in the large majority of Chéret's designs, the pictorial element was seen as having an independent existence: a brand name could be added as required. Typical is one French poster of the period showing a near-naked beauty lying in solitary state in a double bed. On her face is an expression of ineffable happiness as her mind conjures visions of ecstasy. 'Sweet dream...' says the wording above her head—and across the bedclothes the caption concludes '... to own a Kymris bicycle.'

The separate treatment of word and image in the poster of the Belle Époque is a keynote of the period. Even where the wording was not itself an afterthought, it was invariably added to the design as a separate item, more often than not by another hand. It was felt, not entirely without logic, that lettering was a matter for experts, not artists.

It is in this clear division between the two ingredients that the concept of the 1890s poster differs most radically from that of the Second Golden Age, the 1920s and '30s. In its final flowering the poster was to amalgamate the two in an integrated unity; in the meantime, designs continued to be produced in isolation. Taking the matter to its obvious conclusion, many designers produced designs speculatively, drawing in such notional wording as 'Somebody's Jam', 'Blank's Condensed Milk' and the like. The oil painting for 'Blank's Metal Polish' [page 62] is typical of this class of speculative work, carried out on the artist's own initiative and then hawked about for a buyer.

In similar vein, buyers would sometimes advertise for a design; here again the implication was that a pictorial motif might be made to serve any one of a number of brands or products. In March 1900, a London press advertisement invites submissions: 'To artists—wanted, an original design for a poster of a Razor. Preference will be given to a design with an idea in it. Please quote price when sending design.'

It must be said that the Belle Époque, though it was admired and applauded almost everywhere abroad, did not travel well. It certainly failed to cross the Channel. Britain's answer to Chéret was Dudley Hardy, an answer far from convincing. Hardy's Anglo-Saxon version of Gallic effervescence failed to do more than echo the master [page 63]. John Hassall, not quite a serious artist, not quite a postcard vulgarian, remained impervious to the Belle Époque.

In no sense an answer to anybody, but with an impact that stunned the world, was Aubrey Beardsley. His posters were few; like Lautrec, he did them for friends when they came along, but the bulk of his output was a working out of the intricacies of private fantasy. That it was fantasy, in the main, in largely unmentionable terms, was an embarrassment to the majority and the subject of admiring indulgence on the part of the few. Like his contemporary Oscar Wilde, he was a phenomenon of which Britain was by turns proud and deeply ashamed.

Beardsley died of consumption at the age of twenty-five; he left behind him a horrified silence, a few hundred line drawings, many of them of an exquisite nastiness, and a poster or two. Among his best-known posters was the design for T. Fisher Unwin, the publisher [36]. Admirable in its posterly impact, it is related to the subject matter only by the presence in the lady's hand of a book. (The relevance of this voluptuary to the world of children's literature is far from clear. So, too, is the true function of the poster which, in surviving examples, bears neither the name nor the address of the advertiser.)

Saving grace of the Anglo-Saxon scene of the time was the partnership known as the Beggarstaff Brothers. James Pryde and William Nicholson (who were in fact brothers-in-law) joined forces for a brief spell in the middle 1890s to design posters. Each was an established artist in his own right. Neither had produced posters before. Like the complementary packets of a seidlitz powder, they created a new personality.

Renting a cottage in the country, they devoted themselves to an entirely fresh approach to the poster. Using scissors and coloured paper, they produced cut-out shapes and outlines, reducing each pictorial element to the simplest possible statement. The technique was a brilliant success; the partnership, as a commercial venture, was not. Their monuments are very few; a small number of published designs, most of them world famous [44], and a small number of rejected designs, some of them equally so, are all that remain of their brief career. The Beggarstaff phenomenon was perhaps the shortest and most significant episode in poster history.

Fad, Industry—or Menace?

From tentative beginnings late in the nineteenth century, the poster had become a major talking point. All over Europe, and increasingly in the United States, the poster was reaching the status of a cult object. Never before had 'art' become so accessible and understandable. Never before had such distinguished work been so widely seen; these important items, some of them the creation of masters, could almost be peeled off the hoardings and taken home as trophies. As it turned out, they *were* peeled off the hoardings and taken home as trophies.

It was the advent of Toulouse-Lautrec that started the cult of poster collecting. Soon, there had grown up a minor black market in posters; enthusiasts kept watch on bill-stickers and offered them bribes; they bought copies at dusk at contractor's side doors; if all else failed they physically removed them from the walls before the paste was dry.

At one stage, so widespread was the illicit traffic in posters, it became necessary to issue threats. Even Dudley Hardy (who need not, perhaps, have worried) had a notice printed at the foot of his Savoy Theatre posters: 'This poster is the property of Mr R. D'Oyly Carte, London, and any person selling or receiving the same is liable to prosecution.'

The poster became a fad. There were exhibitions of posters and printers of posters (themselves advertised on still more posters) [38,49], poster clubs, poster critics, poster galleries, poster dealers and poster magazines. Serious-mindedness took over. In its first issue *The Poster* said ' . . .l'*affiche* has become an important branch of art, recognised and and patronised not only by those to whom its present prominent position is due, but by all interested in art, from the academician to the curio collector'. The magazine expressed the hope that 'our journal may be a medium by which all can admire and study in the quiet of the home or studio the beauties of the *chef-d'œuvre* of all the hoardings. . .'

In Germany appeared the magazine *Das Plakat*. Soon afterwards, from New York came *The Poster*. Poster appreciation circles and poster exchanges proliferated. Many of them stayed in business; Germany's Society of Friends of the Poster was still circulating a sales list [page 49] in the thick of the 1914–18 war. There were also, it must be recorded, societies of Enemies of the Poster. In Britain, the Society for the Checking of Abuses in Public Advertising came into being in 1892 with the specific intention of doing away with posters altogether. In various countries legislation sought to limit its spread; it was in 1881 that one of France's most publicised laws (since hallowed on every flyposted wall as the *Loi du 29 juillet*) came into force.

The billposting industry, daily gathering strength, was astonished at public objections. In its trade magazines, of which there were by now a number, it expressed itself as shocked, even wounded, by attacks on its activities. The magazines reported with evident pleasure the scale and effectiveness of the industry. The *Bill Poster* describes in 1897 the travelling poster headquarters of Barnum & Bailey's circus: 'The show is preceded on its countrywide tour by five large and elegant advertising cars, each seventy feet long . . . loaded with twenty-five tons of advertising material. Twenty-five bill posters travel with the train. At each town the men leave the train and post their bills. By nightfall the city is bright with beautiful bills. . .'

In the big urban areas, gangs of competing billposters fought with each other as they worked. Said a New York report, 'At 11.30 pm yesterday police were informed that sixty billposters, representing about every theatre in town, were fighting for possession of the facades of 104 and 106 West Thirty-Fourth Street. . .' The trouble was eventually quelled, but not before the combatants had 'hit one another with mucilage mops and beaten tattoos on heads with handles'. It must be admitted that the industry was still at the awkward age.

The turn of the century was the nursery, if not the cradle, of the Consumer Society. Dramatically, inescapably, it brought with it the concept of mass production. The poster, itself a mass product, was not merely evidence of the concept, it was in part its instrument. All over the world the Barnum & Baileys of the industrial scene adopted it. Fresh from the semi-precious days of Chéret and Lautrec, the *affiche* was bundled on to the billboards of the twentieth century.

But the birthplace, Paris, still held on. By now firmly established as a medium for the serious artist, the poster had acquired a solid corpus of glory. Over and above the obvious distinction of Chéret and Lautrec, there were added other notables. Steinlen, Willette, Bonnard, Grasset, Forain—all artists of high repute—had also joined in.

Steinlen started his art career as a painter of cats. His first poster, for an exhibition of his own work, featured his own cats [38]. So did his second, for Guillot Brothers' Sterilised Milk. In this the cats served as supporting cast to his daughter Colette. The poster, printed by Charles Verneau, was a great success. It was also a success in England where, with amendments to the wording, his daughter drank Nestlé's milk [35].

It was Steinlen who designed the poster for posters [49]. The Charles Verneau design is catless, but Colette appears again as a member of the cast among the Paris crowd.

It would be wrong to dismiss Steinlen as a sentimentalist. (Somebody said of him that he was a painter of 'cats, flowers and the poor'.) He had a keen sense of right and wrong and was preoccupied with the injustices, the poverty and inequalities of his time. In his later work, particularly in his posters of 1914–18, his concerns emerge more clearly.

Grasset, also from Switzerland, and another ingredient of the Paris scene, was obsessed with the stained-glass attitudes of the Middle Ages. Much of his poster work was inclined to the heavy outline—an expedient as valid to the poster as to the church window. Grasset preceded Mucha as *affichiste* to Sarah Bernhardt; he also preceded Mucha to the United States, where his poster rendering of Napoleon for a serial in *The Century Magazine* started America collecting posters in earnest.

Grasset, Forain, Bonnard, Willette and the rest—these were the electrons that circled the nucleus of the Paris poster structure. At its heart were Chéret, Toulouse-Lautrec, Steinlen—and Mucha.

Alfons Mucha broke on the poster scene like a roll of tinkling thunder. A foreigner too (classically, cartoonists and poster artists have tended to be foreigners), he brought from his Austro-Hungarian obscurity an idiom hitherto unknown. His poster for Job cigarette papers [40] expresses it in its entirety.

Mucha himself acknowledged a debt to Grasset, and in fact the sensuous outline that characterises most of his work strongly suggests the stained-glass window effect. There is indeed about all his work, even when his subject is cigarette papers, a hint of the high altar. The deity, by and large, was Woman.

His association with Sarah Bernhardt was crucial to his career. Happening by chance to be in a printer's office when the theatre manager telephoned, Mucha was pressed by the printer to go and see her. The outcome of the meeting was a series of posters that was to become, like the lady herself, part of world history. In effecting her apotheosis, he too became immortal.

Starting with *Gismonda* [34] Mucha produced a succession of full-length tributes. Like Chéret before him, he relied on the appeal of his subject's full 150 centimetres. (But he cheated; as her detractors unkindly pointed out, Sarah Bernhardt was noticeably shorter than her poster image.) Sarah was Mucha's subject both in posters for her plays and, it may be suspected, in posters for other things as well. The Bernhardt idea dominated Mucha's world.

The Mucha idea dominated everyone else's world. Throughout the poster scene, in a hundred light disguises, Mucha women appeared as though by magic. The style, with its intertwining tendrils, its outlines and muted tints, became a cult. It spread from posters to interior decor; to furniture, fabrics and the whole gamut of outward appearance. From the suburban porch to the Paris Métro entrance, it served as a universal formula. There are indications that the master himself grew tired of it. Certainly he tired of his own success. In 1903 he took refuge from it all in visits to the United States (where the women, he reported, were 'strong, vigorous—at once svelte and solid . . . large and robust').

His poster career produced much that was significant and much that success forced upon him. Like all his colleagues, he accepted commissions covering a wide range of subjects. He worked for toothpaste firms, makers of chocolates, bath tablets, beer, champagne—and condensed milk. He did two posters for the Nestlé Company—neither of them, it must be said, among his best. The second, designed for the Jubilee of Queen Victoria, bore the words 'Hommage Respectueux de Nestlé'. Set above three portrait roundels of Her Majesty, an unknown female figure held a crown; the figure, though seated, is not absolutely unlike the divine Sarah.

If artists of the distinction of Chéret and Mucha laboured their own themes, lesser lights, who had none of their own, laboured those of their masters. Not only in style but in detail, the rank and file of poster artists plagiarised unashamedly. Who was to know, after all, if Vienna copied Madrid or London copied Paris? With communications still relatively undeveloped, the unscrupulous designer felt safe from discovery. Cribbing became universal. The German poster magazine *Das Plakat*, more watchful and better travelled than the average observer, ran a regular feature on the latest 'lifts', publishing originals and plagiarisms side by side. At one stage, more in despair than anger, the magazine devoted an entire issue to the subject.

The ethics of professional practice among designers had still not been codified; nor had the terms of the Berne Convention on copyright. One Beardsley-style designer in America, having sold a bicycle poster to an American client, removed the bicycles from beneath their seductive riders and substituted desks with typewriters. The result appeared in England as a Beardsley-style poster for the Typewriter Company Limited, Queen Victoria Street, London.

'Pirating' of designs for the collector's market was a factor, too. In November 1898 the editor of *The Poster* warned that an original sketch by the Beggarstaff Brothers had been 'reproduced on the Continent by some unknown persons'. Advising his readers to be on their guard, he added, 'France is decidedly the Mecca for forgeries'.

Though it was the Mecca of so much that concerned the poster, France was not the sole progenitor either of posters or copies. Nor were other centres mere mimics. In Germany and Italy the poster idiom developed along independent lines. The Italian school, led by Metlicovitz, Hohenstein and Dudovich, was cast in the main in a classic mould. For their exhibitions, ceremonial openings and festivals, they tended towards the statuesque, symbolic figure; solo or in elaborate groups, gods, goddesses and acolytes conveyed 'Speed', 'Hygiene', 'Culture'—or whatever was required. The style was also applied to less exalted subjects; Hohenstein's harvest allegory *Birra Italia* [45] is typical; further down the scale, the anti-seasickness belt design [28] imposed a strain on the observer's suspension of disbelief.

The style also imposed strains on a respectable sense of the fitness of things. Censorship, which had now moved firmly into the field of sexual morals, disliked nudity, classical or otherwise. More than one such Italian poster found itself formally obliged to go and put some pants on quickly. To the advertiser who had to reprint the amended design the operation was costly. To the bill poster, who was liable to prosecution for indecent exposure, the whole business was frightening: 'It behoves advertisers,' breathed *The Bill Poster* through clenched teeth, 'to be especially discriminating as to anything approaching indelicacy. . .'

In Germany, the first twitchings of *Jugendstil* (Germany's version of *art nouveau*) were felt at an early stage. Otto Fischer, with his Beggarstaff-cum-Mucha treatment of his Dresden exhibition poster [39], was recognisably close to the centre. So, too, was Emil Weiss, and though he produced only a single poster, so was Henry van de Velde, Weimar's proponent of *art nouveau*.

It was van de Velde who, as director of the Weimar School of Arts and Crafts, later appointed Walter Gropius as head of the revolutionary new design school, the 'Bauhaus'. His choice was to prove historic.

As to the rest of Europe there was little of note to report: Spain, Portugal, Holland,

Austria-Hungary and Scandinavia offered for the most part a pale reflection of the Paris scene. Only in Belgium, where Privat Livemont held sway, was there more than competence. But here, too, objective judgement must recognise a debt—a heavy debt—to Mucha; the 'Belgian School' was in reality the school of Mucha/Livemont. In Holland there was J. G. van Caspel [48]. Spain offered Alejandro de Riquer (an Iberian Mucha/Grasset). The rest was irrelevance.

The poster hit America in 1894. With startling suddenness (and with the importation of a consignment of European posters) the cult of the Belle Époque was swallowed whole. The names of Chéret, Toulouse-Lautrec and Mucha became cultural war cries.

The collecting craze, in Europe a pleasant pastime for gentlemen, in America became a paper chase. When Sarah Bernhardt brought her own actual Mucha posters, and Eugene Tompkins advertised a play with real Chéret designs, excitement ran high.

Of all of the imports however, none was so frenziedly received as the spirit of Aubrey Beardsley. The Englishman, Scotson-Clark, a refugee from the respectability of Brighton, England, and himself a poster artist, writes in *The Poster* for November 1900, 'Until the winter of 1894, the artistic poster was practically unknown in the United States. The only things of the kind, and they were very excellent and very original, were the *Harper's Magazine* window bills by Edward Penfield. But during the latter part of 1893, and the early half of 1894, the name and work of Aubrey Beardsley had become known, and popular as was his success amongst a large class in England, his fame was tenfold in America. Every twopenny-halfpenny town had its 'Beardsley' artist, and the large cities simply teemed with them. Some borrowed his ideas and adapted them to their own uses; others imitated, till one asked oneself: "Is this done by the English or the American B?"'

Bradley was the name of the best-known American B—Will H. Bradley. His window-bill for the magazine *The Chap Book* [37] epitomises the position. Other American artists were influenced by other names. Edward Penfield, of whom Scotson-Clark approved, was much impressed by Toulouse-Lautrec. Maxfield Parrish, Louis Rhead (another expatriate Briton), Ethel Reed and the rest also pursued paths which were not outstandingly original.

By the turn of the century American factories were producing drawing-room screens bearing the decorative 'Four Seasons' panels of Mucha. The American Belle Époque had come and almost gone. Percival Pollard, referring to the popularity of the Mucha screens, writes, 'It is true that the public, buying these screens, is mostly unaware of their inspiration, but if posters can educate the general art feeling, even by stealth, so much the better. . .'

The American landscape, nurtured on the concept of the outsize billboard, had second thoughts about the *affiche*. As the twentieth century began to unfold, it took up again where it had left off. The Parrishes and Penfields moved back to their earlier work as magazine and book illustrators and decorative artists. The age of Leyendecker, Christy, Flagg and Charles Dana Gibson was yet to come.

'Your Country Needs You'

By the end of its first decade, the twentieth century had shown that the Consumer Society was a going concern. Mass production, mass markets and mass communications had arrived. The conveyor belt, the assembly line, the transport network, the printed word—these were the perfectly inter-operating instruments of the New Age, elements in an apparently limitless cycle of increasing supply and increasing demand. Mass production had become a concept worthy of development almost for its own sake.

By the time the war in Europe had moved into its first winter, the proposition stood neatly on its head. On a scale hitherto unimagined (and also operating in apparently limitless cycles of supply and demand) destruction now took over. The poster, not least of the tools of mass technology, achieved a new status. It turned from selling the comforts of peace to pressing the demands of war. In numbers, if not obviously in quality, it gathered strength.

Its adoption was not always immediate, nor was the pattern of its use necessarily the same among all the belligerents. In Britain, where in the first months of the war there was no conscription, the accent was initially on recruitment alone. Even in this there had been some reluctance; could an army be raised by *advertising for one*? (And even if it could, was it proper to do so? The Germans themselves, incredulous at such military folly, were additionally dubious as to the dignity of the procedure; said one enemy critic, 'Should an army be raised by the same means as customers for jam?')

In January 1914 *The Times*, announcing a press advertising campaign for recruits, and expressing the slight sense of distaste that the topic aroused, said that 'the campaign . . . or the first move in it, is apparently to extend over a week, and to be carried on through such newspapers as are likely to fall into the hands of the class to which the appeal is particularly addressed'.

Distasteful or not, by the year's end some millions of men faced each other across the Western Front and the small press campaign had become a poster campaign. Under the aegis of a Parliamentary Recruiting Committee a series of posters appeared—most of them very poor, some of them distinctly bad. Notorious for their mawkish sentiment and style, some of these have remained uneasily in the memory ever since. In one design a post-war child enquires of his obviously civilian father, '*Daddy, what did you do in the war?*' In another a mother and her children gaze bravely through a window as menfolk march off to the front; the caption: *Women of Britain Say GO!*

It was in Alfred Leete's Lord Kitchener, *Your Country Needs YOU* [61], that the British war poster came somewhere near greatness. The basic idea, relying for its effect on the dominance of the father-figure and the inescapability of the pointing finger, sparked off posters everywhere; from hoardings in Italy, Russia and Austria-Hungary fingers pointed mercilessly. In the United States, over the signature of James Montgomery Flagg, Uncle Sam also pointed. '*I Want you for US Army*' [59], he said, and allowed space for the address of the nearest recruiting station. (Not bothering to point, but no less challengingly, Howard Christy's transvestite girl [58] competed by claiming the viewer for the Navy.)

The saving grace of the British war poster scene was Frank Brangwyn, printer, lithographer and student of the common man. Brangwyn brought to the medium not only competence but a sense of deep conviction. His renderings of war scenes, particularly of refugee evacuation in Belgium and rescue of survivors at sea, have absolute authority. Unlike most of his contemporaries, he was incapable of idealising the war; his wounded are real wounded, his war is war.

The Brangwyn approach found little favour among the Establishment. Some found his posters 'quite unsuitable'. Not only were they too 'artistic', they had the demerit, according to one critic, of 'showing the seamy side of war'.

At a period when shortage of lithographic stone had brought in zinc as a substitute (a change that was to become permanent), Brangwyn still worked on stone. Like his contemporary, Spenser Pryse, who humped lithographic stone from place to place in the war-zone by motorcar, his was the muscular, raw-boned approach of the dedicated artist. Like many others, he moved into the field of posters and moved out again. There were to be later Brangwyn posters, such as the famous *Zambrene* design [90], but they were few.

America's version of Britain's Parliamentary Recruitment Committee was the Division of Pictorial Publicity, a group more expert, more productive, but equally multi-headed and diffuse. In a valedictory book distributed to its members in 1919, the division was congratulated not only on its war effort but on its artistic example: 'The steady appearance of the Division's work became a feature of the war, not only stirring patriotism but awakening in the public mind the importance of the artist. It was a wholesale education to the country in that the Division made the billboards safe for art, the work standing out in sharp contrast to the commercial disfigurations of the past.' It must be judged that the commercial disfigurations of the past were bad indeed. America's output of war posters, though plentiful, was also undistinguished.

The Division of Pictorial Publicity was launched not by 'the authorities' but by artists themselves. Charles Dana Gibson, originator of the famed 'Gibson Girl', called his artist colleagues together at a dinner in New York in April 1917. As one man the group offered its services, free of charge, to the US Government. As one man the US Government accepted.

There was forthwith established a procedure which was to remain in operation until the war's end: the whole group met once a week to be briefed in the propaganda needs of various government departments, the fighting forces and other 'clients'. Their requests were read out to the assembled artists. Says W. S. Rogers in his *Book of the Poster*, 'Each request was put in charge of a "captain" whose duty it was to see that idea-sketches were received, on time, from such of the artists as were best fitted to carry out the work. These idea-sketches were then passed through Committee Headquarters to Washington and, when approved, were promptly executed in finished paintings.'

For all its obvious disadvantages, the system was an improvement on the British plan. In London, war poster ideas were often originated by whoever happened to think of one, and then, after on-the-nod approval from the head of a department, finished off by the nearest artist. The Gibson Committee at least maintained some sort of contact with its clientele.

The American view of poster campaigns was markedly statistical; production facts and figures were quoted almost with the weight of military victories. 'The activity of the Division of Pictorial Publicity', said one writer, 'needs no proof beyond the figures of its output. Seven hundred posters were made to serve the publicity demands of fifty government and civilian war needs.' It was claimed that in the nineteen months of its existence the group notched up a total ('inclusive of banners, window cards and other publicity material') of 1,484 designs.

There was no lack of quantity. Quality on the other hand, as in Britain, was another matter. If the 'poster artist' was only a recent arrival in Britain, in America he was virtually non-existent. The men who answered Dana Gibson's call were illustrators, portrait painters and fine artists; for each one of them it was a case of 'having a go at a poster'. With little to guide them but instinct—and the reactions of their Government clients—they learnt as they went along.

A quick learner was James Montgomery Flagg. His 'Uncle Sam' design was to prove 'the war's most successful all-purpose bill'. So successful was it that, on the strength of it, Flagg stopped going to Gibson's weekly meetings. He had in any case had an overdose of poster patriotics: 'I soon became horribly bored with rising toasts,' he said. His 'Uncle Sam' (for which, suitably attired, he himself posed at a mirror) was destined to have a re-run in World War II—and modified reappearances in the late 1960s [page 103]. Altogether, the two wars are said to have accounted for printings of a total of 4 million copies; later reprints may bring the grand total to 5 million. Appearing as a magazine cover for *Leslie's Illustrated*, the original poster, like Leete's Kitchener design, has become part of a national heritage—a key-image for two, and even three, generations.

Howard Chandler Christy, another 'non-poster artist', scored a big success with his female naval officer and *Americans All!* [57], a design not far removed from the set-piece style of turn-of-the-century Rome [28]. Other names to appear as signatures on United States posters were R. J. Wildhack, C. B. Falls, Henry Reuterdahl, J. C. Leyen-decker, Charles Dana Gibson himself, and even 'fine artist' Joseph Pennell, with a shape-of-things-to-come vision of an air raid on New York.

Poster techniques in Europe, already in advance of those in the United States in 1914, had developed significantly in the early years of the war. Working on the foundations laid by the pioneers, second and third generations of artists had begun to develop a new approach—the specifically 'poster' style which was to inform the medium throughout its adult life. The poster was now conceived not just as a pasted-up picture but as a graphic device in its own right. The poster designer, though still recruited from other fields, began to be viewed as a specialist. The 'Bubbles' age was finally over.

The new approach had been foreshadowed twenty years before, brilliantly but briefly, by the Beggarstaffs. Using the simplest of tone and colour masses, and omitting all unnecessary detail, their technique relied for its impact on an irreducible minimum of graphic effort. The fine detail and delicate gradations of the oil painting or colour lithograph had given way to a treatment at once more commanding and more quickly understood. The effect was described (for the first time, and significantly) by the new-coined adjective *postery*.

Ludwig Hohlwein's first posters appeared in Germany in 1906. Unlike the Beggarstaffs, he 'caught on'. By 1914, though still working largely in Germany, he was part of the European scene. His influence and his work were to remain part of the scene until the late 1940s.

His internee exhibition poster [62] sums him up. Among the dozen or so poster artists who realised the need for simplicity, Hohlwein was one of the few who saw virtue in apparent disadvantage. The tempo of life had increased and (not least in wartime) there was neither time nor inclination to stop and admire: for the public, the poster was a matter of the briefest of passing impressions. Hohlwein's economy of treatment had the effect not merely of speeding recognition—it added immeasurably to graphic impact. In addition, whereas earlier forms of simplification had tended to produce a two-dimensional effect, Hohlwein's analysis rendered its subjects in the round; his figures were not patterns cut out of coloured paper, they were real.

Unlike his predecessors of the Belle Époque who were inclined to view the designing of a poster as an opportunity for the entertainment of the artist, Hohlwein saw it as a challenging job of work. For him it was the *message* that mattered; the poster was an instrument, not a decoration. In this, as in much else, Hohlwein may be considered as the father of the poster in its twentieth-century sense.

Poster themes in wartime, geared at first mainly to appeals for war-loan subscriptions, moved rapidly through the gamut: next came calls for help for the fighting man, for help for the wounded, for aid to refugees, orphans and widows. Then, at the scraping of the bottom of the barrel, for one last superhuman effort.

Behind their respective frontiers poster campaigns exhorted, cajoled and threatened; the similarity, not only of their respective messages but also sometimes of their designs, was remarkable. There were occasions when virtually the same poster, differentiated only by language, did duty for both sides at once. Forged in the same fire, the poster instrument became universalised. The gradual sharpening of poster know-how began to produce a universal idiom, a trend that in the end was to merge into one overall graphic pattern—the image of the 1920s.

The majority of people thought that peace would restore the world to 'normal'—to the way it had been before 1914. But there were many who saw that the world would never be the same again. The convulsion of the war, social revolution, economic chaos—

not to mention a total of 37 million casualties—all were mirrored in the manners and modes of the new decade. So was the march of mass technology. The posters ˆ the 1920s were different from their predecessors not only in style but in content. There were posters for petrol, for motorcars and accessories, there were travel posters, rail, road, sea and even airways posters. With the arrival of the moving picture, entertainment had become an industry: there were film posters. Mass-market products like soap, confectionery and drink, once reckoned in their tens of thousands, now moved into the millions. The advertising machine, previously an *ad hoc* contraption, devised by the managing director himself, was rebuilt to a new design by specialists. The conveyor belts—of productivity and promotion alike—slipped into higher gear.

The Second Golden Age

The history of poster design in the 1920s and '30s is dominated by two great names: E. McKnight Kauffer and A. Mouron Cassandre. Hard on their heels came the other immortals—the older Hohlwein and contemporaries Colin, Carlu, Purvis and Austin Cooper—but effectively the inter-war years belong, in France to Cassandre, and in Britain to Kauffer. Each brought to the medium a new and distinctive offering; each in his own lifetime became a legend.

Adolphe Jean-Marie Mouron, alias A. M. Cassandre, was born in Kharkov in 1901 and started working in Paris in the early twenties. Among his first commissions was a poster for a cloth-cap manufacturer; even with the least promising of subjects his freshness of outlook and his keen sense of visual impact singled him out as unique. In a long and fertile series he proved not merely a master of the idiom of the poster, he was in some measure its inventor.

His poster for the *Étoile du Nord* [98], geometric, non-pictorial but full of a breathless visual zest, spotlights a high-point in his career. In the same year (1927) on a similar topic in different mood, he came up with the *Bestway* poster for the London, Midland & Scottish Railway [100]. Against the background of his contemporaries, with their literal-minded pictorialism, their addiction to landscapes, bathing belles and all the rest of the standard paraphernalia, this work was different. Here was not just the 'eccentricity' of the '20s, here was a new and impressive graphic form. Cassandre went from strength to strength. His comic-strip poster for Dubonnet [118] became world-famous. His poster for Prunier's new restaurant in London (1936) [125] is a collector's classic. With Cassandre, the mechanics of the poster reached a new pitch of refinement: if Hohlwein had lifted the poster from the level of decor, Cassandre lifted it to the status of a communications medium.

The impact of E. McKnight Kauffer, less geometric, freer and easier in style, was as unmistakable and as individual. Here again there was a complete dismissal of precedent —an approach to the poster as though none had previously existed. The Stonehenge poster (*See Britain First on Shell*) [120] owes nothing to anyone—not even Cassandre. It is a simple statement, as personal as a signature, direct, compelling and engaging.

Like Hohlwein before him, and many others after him, Kauffer was also interested in the poster potential of photography. His use of the camera was sparing and deliberate; the BP Ethyl design [119] (carefully signed: *Photographed and designed by E. McKnight Kauffer*) is a superb example of his stage-management of the medium.

Kauffer constructed a poster world of his own. He opened new visual avenues, and invited the public to join him. It must be said that, initially at least, there was no great rush to join him; the guardians of the public taste—those whose job it was to commission posters from artists—were dubious. Kauffer epitomised the 'modern' style; the British public, nurtured on Hassall's Skegness approach [73] (and never having really forgotten Sir John Millais' grandson), were suspicious. For his introduction to the public, Kauffer was indebted to Frank Pick, administrator, visionary and poster-watcher for London's Underground Railways. Pick, who rose to become vice-chairman of the London Passenger Transport Board, was a man of great insight; he combined administrative ability with a keen eye for graphic art. He was 'the first great industrialist and the first great businessman to apply the principles of good design to every detail and every activity of a great undertaking'. He was also the first man to recognise E. McKnight Kauffer.

It was Pick who, during the blackest months of 1916, had commissioned lettering artist Edward Johnston to design a new typeface for all London Transport's announcements and notices; it was Pick who called in Epstein, Gill and Henry Moore to produce sculpture for the new headquarters building in 1929; Pick who, often in the face of opposition, and by his own judgement alone, was to be responsible for the launching of many of the great names of the poster.

It has been said that there were three major design influences at work in Europe between the wars: one was Walter Gropius, another was Jack Beddington, who commissioned posters for Shell; the third was Frank Pick.

In fairness to his competitors, it must be said however that Pick's espousal of the graphic arts was less than onerous. No one judged the success of London Transport posters by the traffic turnover of the time: only rarely were they regarded as messages more compelling than a passing greeting to the traveller on his way. In this one context, deep below the streets of London, the poster still clung to its former role; the 'hard sell' of the wider world was absent.

London Transport was to retain its 'soft-sell' role throughout the years. There were phases when, far from encouraging increased custom, it pleaded with people to ease off a bit. For those who ignored the call, packing themselves in ever more tightly, London Transport's posters served merely as an antidote to claustrophobia.

With Frank Pick's help—perhaps even because of it—the '20s and '30s brought the Second Golden Age of the British poster. The old masters, pictorialists like Frank Newbould [75], Fred Taylor and Charles Pears still reigned, and there were the new names, men who had, if not the Kauffer view, the Kauffer sense of reappraisal. Among them in the earlier part of the period, emerged Ashley Havinden, Pat Keely, Tom Purvis and Austin Cooper.

In a company of the great, Austin Cooper was supreme. His work for London Transport, for London museums and exhibitions and for the national railway companies embodied the poster concept at its best.

His forte was in the selection and presentation of the evocative image. *Paris for the Weekend* [103] is one of a set of three commissioned by the Southern Railway in 1934, a series designed for display on railway platforms. Of them Cooper wrote, 'Where passengers already knew something of the places advertised they might perhaps, or so I thought, be made to feel slightly nostalgic—sufficiently so to consider once again sampling a flask of chianti in the Piazza San Marco, a café crème or a Pernod, in the Boule' Miche.' Cooper's modest exercise in nostalgia was to prove a poster landmark of the middle 1930s.

Although he was a master of montage Cooper was equally successful in the bold use of the 'single image'. His poster for the *Foire de Paris* [129] is a classic of its kind. In the full perspective of poster history, Cooper's contribution must be seen as close to the very peak of the Second Golden Age. He stands vis-à-vis Kauffer in London as Jean Carlu to Cassandre in Paris.

In France, the 1920s' golden age was still outshone by the afterglow of the turn of the century. There was Jean Carlu [109], who was to be a key figure for a quarter of a century. There were also Jacques Nathan, Charles Loupot, and Francis Bernard. But for the moment, at least, much of the focus of poster excitement centred on London.

In Germany, Ludwig Hohlwein stayed at the top. Close behind were the other elders: Lucian Bernhard, Julius Gipkens, Fritz Gotha [76], Hans Rosen [87], Engelhardt and Julius Klinger. New boys were 'Trias' (Rolf Frey) student of Julius Klinger, Willy Petzold [124] and Jupp Wiertz [70].

In Dessau, Walter Gropius, having bowed to the disapproval of the citizens of Weimar, set up his new Bauhaus. From here, until its closure by the National Socialist Government, it continued its increasing influence, not only on graphic design but on the whole spectrum of art, architecture and industrial design. It was already an international influence before its closure; with its enforced emigration in 1933 the Bauhaus philosophy spread throughout the world.

Gropius called for an end to the airs and graces of pointless decoration; he sought a complete break with the clichés and conceits of the past. Returning to first principles, he encouraged a simplistic approach to design, with a complete reappraisal of the nature of its problems. The graphic artist, like the architect, the town planner and the industrial designer, took heed.

But the Gropius revolution, sweeping as it was, left pockets of resistance. In Italy, for example, the going was hard. Marcello Nizzoli [115], Lucio Venna [82] and a number of others moved with the new impetus. For the most part, however, there was still a hankering for the old-time pictorialism, the set-piece grandiosities of Plinio Codognato [93] and Leopoldo Metlicovitz [77].

In the United States, too, response was sluggish. With publicity budgets now firmly geared to the dominance of commercial radio, and the tradition of the wide-screen billboard solidly entrenched, America had grown accustomed to its own outdoor graphics. By and large the big bills were not true posters; effectively they were panoramic adaptations of illustrated magazine advertisements. Ignoring the visual shorthand of the European approach, the billboard served in the main as background support to the spoken word. In one development, in which a basic design was made available for overprinting by a trader in a given locality [84], there was some concession to the mainstream poster concept, but on the whole it must be said that America's billboards had changed little, either in matter or manner, from the early days of 1919. Even in the film poster— a potentially fertile field for development—things stayed very much the same. The *Bolero* design [117] is exceptional; its billboard neighbours in 1932 were crowded, cluttered and overblown. The general formula was an amalgam of Goldwyn and Barnum & Bailey. It remained virtually unchanged into the '70s.

The '20s and early '30s saw increasing use of the poster in social issues. In Germany particularly, social and political pressures expressed themselves. There were appeals and counter-appeals, claims and counter-claims. Käthe Kollwitz, in her *Berliner Winterhilfe* design [80] graphically imparts the urgencies of the times.

Soviet Russia's poster output increased. Hard on the heels of the scores of posters put out at the time of the revolution itself, the aftermath brought a second wave. In nicely balanced proportions, poster campaigns combined exhortation, instruction and imprecation. By the standards of today some of these designs have an old-fashioned air. The 'Come-into-Public-Life' appeal to women [113] has a wooden, self-conscious look. On the other hand, the anti-clerical/capitalist design of D. S. Moor, *Proletarians, Be on Your Guard!* [94] is aggressively alive. It has all the ingredients of the modern propaganda poster, a commanding, simple treatment, and a commanding message.

D. S. Moor (Dimitri Stakheyevitch Orlov) was the outstanding Russian poster artist of his time. Working in an atmosphere of change and turmoil, virtually isolated from the design concepts of the outside world and fiercely dedicated to the cause, he produced posters that ring with conviction. This quality, so obviously missing at the commercial level, can raise poster design to great heights. It is the studio, so to speak, to the sound of gunfire.

In the posters of the Spanish designers in the Civil War of 1936–39 the same quality appeared. As it happens, almost all of the surviving specimens are from the Government side, but whatever the observer's personal view, their impact is inescapable. The sense of strength and unity in the *People's Army* design [123], conveyed with a minimum of effort, is overwhelming. Designed and produced sometimes literally to the sound of gunfire, the posters of a civil war fit oddly into a Golden Age. But there can be no doubt that 1936–39, whatever else it brought, brought this much gold as well.

Switzerland was the dark horse of the 1920s poster world; she had begun by the 1930s to move out on her own. The poster, encouraged by a lively printing industry and by a no less lively government interest, became almost overnight a national sport. The country's geographic situation, a centre of internationality, brought the design trends of Europe to a focal point. The advantages of good printing, rational display, clear air and official encouragement shortly made Switzerland a poster country. Artists like Augusto Giacometti [104], Herbert Matter [112], Ernst Keller [106], Alois Carigieti and Max Bill became international names.

It was at this time, too, that Walter Herdeg appeared. Poster designer and doyen of connoisseurs, his graphics journals and publications became world authorities. The Government's annual poster competition, a major national event, set Switzerland's seal permanently on the art, craft, cult and industry of the poster. From the ignominy of seventeenth-century flyposting, the *affiche* had come, in one country at least, to full official status.

In Britain, as tensions in Europe mounted, the poster scene was enriched by transfusions. F. H. K. Henrion, Hans Schleger, Jan Le Witt, George Him, Stan Krol, Dorrit Dekk and Hans Unger were among those who moved to London in the 1930s. Their names were to become familiar, not only in Britain, but throughout the world.

'Take Cover at Once'

Unlike the 1914–18 war, when the press and the poster had been the major communications media, World War II relied for its public contact chiefly on radio. The poster, though it had proliferated enormously in the years between, played a relatively minor role. There was no frenzied spilling-out of poster ideas, no Parliamentary Committee or Gibson Group. In overall propaganda strategy the poster in most countries served simply as a support service to radio information.

Poster coverage was understandably patchy. In occupied territories posters were produced (by victors and vanquished alike) under varying degrees of stress. There was clandestine production by the occupied, and enforced production by the intruder. (*Germans Out!*—an 'Italian' poster [138] was, in fact, printed by the American Office of War Information; the Italian appeal for loyalty to Mussolini [135] was printed by the Germans.) In unoccupied areas the poster spectrum ranged from the ridiculous (*In an Air Raid Don't Stand and Look at the Sky; Take Cover at Once*) to the sublime: *Don't Betray my Son!* [136].

If the overall picture is ragged, two or three points stand out clearly. In Italy the undoubted master was Gino Boccasile; among a population of wavering morale his mourning mother figure [136] made a deep and lasting impression. In Germany, Hohlwein still held on [133] and in the United States, the war's most powerful poster came from a Frenchman, Jean Carlu, [132] who happened to find himself in America as his country was overrun. In Britain there was significant work from Jan Le Witt and George Him (Lewitt-Him) and from Pat Keely, F. H. K. Henrion, Reginald Mount and a number of others, but few would dispute that on balance it was Abram Games' war.

Abram Games was twenty-three when he joined the army as a private in the infantry. Already a poster designer of note, he observed the need for posters in the army, and said so. Of his own initiative he sketched out a few ideas (one of them, born of shocked acquaintance with the barrack room, stressed the need for clean feet); within a short time he was withdrawn from the barrack room and installed, with full military honours, as official poster artist in an upper room at the War Office.

His first war poster was captioned *Keep your Feet Clean!* and was signed *A. Games, RE*. He was the first Royal Engineer to appear in four-colour litho. He designed over a hundred posters, among them the most memorable of the war. His subjects ranged over the whole field of war service, civilian and military. Unlike many of his predecessors (and many of his contemporaries), he was not content merely to pictorialise. Each poster was a well-aimed shaft—a clarifying 'diagram', a visual *double-entendre* or a mnemonic image.

'Careless talk', a security hazard for all the belligerents, was the subject of posters all over the world. Games himself did half-a-dozen on the theme. But there can be little doubt that *Your Talk May Kill Your Comrades* [134] stands supreme. Here is the 'diagram' approach, the unmistakable message with its horrifying image of cause and effect, a presentation dramatic, compelling and memorable.

From his room at the War Office Abram Games set new standards in the technique of the propaganda poster.

Britain's wartime graphics, both in the field of posters and in exhibitions and displays, were noticeably better than their pre-war counterparts. Here again, the designer with a cause was seen to do better than his commercial *alter ego*. The problem, after it was all over, was to do as well for peace. There was also another problem, and it was Games who stated it: the poster masters of the past, brilliant as they were, had tended to specialise in the soft-sell fields, the relatively undemanding areas of travel, transport, prestige and the like. They had relied on the distinctive treatment of surface and the stylising of figures, landscape and lettering. Could the poster penetrate more deeply; could it, as it had done in wartime, actually *persuade*?

The Poster Goes to Pieces

What commercial radio had done to the poster in the United States in the '30s and '40s, commercial television tended to do in Europe in the '50s and '60s. It would be untrue to say that the poster came to a sudden stop; there were many areas in which it carried on as usual. In 'good works' for example [141], in relief and reconstruction [140, 142], in public services [156] and safety campaigns [144]. In all these sectors the wartime impetus continued. But for mainstream advertising of mass-market products, commercial television began to take over. It is not without significance that Games, in one of his early peace-time commercial posters [143], extolled the medium that was to have such a profound effect upon his own.

With one or two exceptions the 'mainline' designers began to revert to their former role as servants of the soft-sell, finding their clients among airlines, public services and organisers of exhibitions and festivals. Among these there was notable work in Britain from Stan Krol, Tom Eckersley, Leonard Cusden and Harry Stevens; in France from Jean Colin and Jacques Nathan; in Germany from Alexander Wagner and Michael Engelmann; Switzerland: Herbert Leupin and Donald Brun; Italy: Erberto Carboni and Alfredo Lalia; United States: Josef Binder and Paul Rand, and in Poland: Waldemar Swierzy and Wojciech Zomecznik.

Apart from the work of these, poster design galloped off in all directions at once. One development, pursued to some effect by Charles Loupot in France in the late '50s, became an international talking-point. Loupot took the well-known name-block and colour scheme of the aperitif 'St Raphaël', restyled it, chopped it into fragments and scattered it as a pattern over the hoardings. The effect [page 100] was memorable.

But for the majority of advertisers in the mass-consumer field the poster designer, as such, virtually ceased to exist. The poster became a mere addendum to a television campaign: sometimes so completely was the poster integrated with the TV concept, it was incomprehensible to anyone who had failed to see the basic campaign on the screen.

Television exerted another pressure: for audiences accustomed to the 'photographic' quality of the TV image, the idiom of the conventional poster began to lose point. A photographic treatment, whether in black and white or in colour, related more readily to the television presentation, evoking its full message in a single picture. Photography moved in on the poster. Sometimes the image was an actual frame from the commercial [163]; sometimes, in a curiously circular process of implication, there was even a photographic evocation of the viewing situation itself [167]. In some cases authorship of the poster was credited to a single individual, as in Cremonesi's 'Keep-Milan-Tidy' design [165]; in others, as in the Swiss sunglasses example [166], credits were divided, sometimes between photographer and art director, sometimes in a three-way split to include the copywriter.

With the advent of the photographic poster the movement towards 'design by teamwork', already widely accepted by post-war advertising agencies, came to its full development.

Many of the pictures thus produced were superb examples of their kind, not only from a photographic point of view but as feats of graphic reproduction. The Martell Brandy example [164] is a masterpiece from any point of view. The picture, in its choice of models, in the adroitness of its composition and in its evocation of atmosphere, succeeds splendidly. But for all that, the 'conventional' poster designer views the style with mistrust. 'C'est magnifique,' he murmurs, 'mais ce n'est pas l'affiche.'

However strong the pressure from the camera-men, the '50s and '60s still held room for the initiative of the designer. If the poster was suspected of having passed its peak, Abram Games, for one, was not. Nor was Savignac.

Raymond Savignac was a one-man renaissance. A master of irreverence, and of an uncompromising Gallic logic, he gave every subject in every poster a new—and yet obvious—twist. His designs for milk-soap [155], and the Cologne Carnival [159] are examples from an apparently inexhaustible supply of good humour.

Outside Europe there were poster trends in various directions, some of them new, some of them not. In the People's Republic of China the poster (here also, reputedly produced by teamwork) loomed large. Two styles were apparent, both of them 'un-Chinese' to Western eyes. In one there is an echo of Hollywood 1950; in the other [153] an echo of Hollywood 1940. In each there is a crowded, colourful sense of occasion— a continuous, super-colossal wide-screen Happening.

Cuba is another poster world on its own. Here, in a remarkable flowering of virtuosity, a new and dynamic drive emerges. In the work of Felix Beltrán [page 100], Peña, Rostgaard and others, a revolution has produced a revolution. Again there is the fire of personal dedication, the thrust and power of conviction and committedness. It seems just possible (but only just) that if the poster's present fragmentation is to be halted, Cuba might be a good place to start afresh.

The Reprographic Revolution

A less restricted world on its own is the world of protest. The techniques of mass production, no less advanced in the field of the image than in other mass technology, have become increasingly available to the individual members of the mass market. Image reproduction, in words or pictures or both, has moved from the printing plant to the office and living-room table. The transition, one of the least-recognised yet possibly one of the most significant developments in human history, has given every individual opinion a new dimension. Now no longer a passive recipient of the products of the presses, the ordinary man is his own publisher.

The coming of the do-it-yourself reprographic processes, of simple silkscreen printing, of the small photolitho printing press and the lettering transfer systems, has brought a sudden explosion of self-expression. Not least among its many forms is the do-it-yourself poster.

The phenomenon has been two-fold: there is an awakening not only to the potentials of the new processes but also to earlier neglected ones; the cut-out stencil, the wood- and lino-cut, have been rediscovered too.

The stencil, cut with a knife from card or thin metal, allows multiple copies to be made from one simple original. All that is needed is a surface to print on and ink or paint for the image. The image must necessarily be simple; it must be contrived so that cutting does not cause the whole structure to fall to pieces. The wood- or lino-cut has advantages in that it remains in one piece no matter how intricate the design; but here there is the disadvantage that the design, together with any lettering, must be carried out in reverse so that it appears the right way round when printed. In screen printing, an intricately cut stencil is prevented from falling to pieces by a fine mesh support. Paint or ink is squeegeed through the mesh to the printing surface.

The three processes have predominated in the graphics of protest. They are the first resort of the 'underground poster press' and the student poster workshop [157, 169, 172, 173]. In May 1968, when Paris students barricaded themselves in their college buildings, these were the techniques that produced some hundreds of different designs—many of them in overnight printings—for placarding all over the capital. (It must be recorded that in at least one of these, originating as a lino-cut, the artist failed to remember to render the design in reverse. The printed result, although reading back-to-front was duly posted up with the rest. The rectified design, redrawn and reprinted, appeared shortly afterwards [page 103].)

Second line of approach for *ad hoc* graphics has been the small litho press, a scaled-down version of the commercial printer's big machines. Here the designer prepares a single black and white original. Often it is composed by pasting down photographs and adding press-on transfer lettering; sometimes the work is the designer's original art-work. The result is photographed on to zinc plates for litho printing.

In the main, it may be doubted that the poster has much benefited from this popular adoption. In a few cases, urgency and the limitations of the techniques have combined to produce notable work. For the most part, even where designs have been produced by art students, results have been noticeably poor. Not least in the defects has been a certain incoherence, both visual and textual. It is perhaps surprising that spelling and grammar, not normally a subject of poster appraisal, should also fall short of ordinary educated levels.

Over and above considerations of the poster on its own—of its levels of design, literacy and execution—the reprographic revolution has implications on a broader scale. The old syndrome of censorship, control and clandestine production must necessarily reappear. Regardless of the political colour of the Establishment, the clamp-down of the fifteenth and sixteenth centuries, the hunting and harrying of 'illicit' operators, becomes a virtual certainty. It must also be seen that the reprographic society is a challenge not only to the existing order; in post-revolutionary situations, too, it remains a challenge—to the new regime. The cycle may be infinitely repeated.

A further point may be noticed: the process whereby the power of reproduction of the printed image has now become available to the individual must inevitably be repeated in other media. As with all technology, the do-it-yourself level has no foreseeable limits. The electronic message, already freely available as 'walkie-talkie' transmission and as tape in sound and vision, will be no more readily confinable than print production.

Parallel with protest there has been the trend to 'pop'. In its own way this may be seen as a backlash movement, a reversal of the traditional flow from the presses to the masses. The cult, with its outlines, sunbursts and colouring-book techniques, rejects the tired clichés of the Establishment, and substitutes its own. With its concomitant side-shows of psychedelia and hallucinogenics, it offers relief from the 'broad grin' of the old world of advertising, a world which Abram Games has earlier categorised as itself an escape from reality. As a communications medium, however, it may leave something to be desired. With the cross-fertilisation of pop and protest there has emerged an idiom, contrived or accidental, of convoluted non-communication. The effect, broadly speaking, is personal, private—a multicoloured rendering of individual inner tensions.

It must be said at once that a mixture of incoherence and illegibility produces posters of limited application. As 'posters', their chief outlet has been the pop gallery and the novelty shop. But their influence has been seen in the ordinary commercial field; just as protest achieved its modest recognition from industry [168], pop and psychedelia have been adopted, too [170, 175]. The effect offers little promise of a bright future.

There has, however, been one major growth point. Recording companies, taking their cue from the success of the genre as applied to the pop record sleeve, have developed their own poster cult. Neglecting the commercial sites, they employ the turn-of-the-century flyposting technique. Pasted and over-pasted on empty shop fronts and un-official frontages, their individual complexities merge in an overall confusion. Some of the designs, more than ordinarily arcane, are inadvertently pasted upside down or sideways [page 102].

The poster gallery, as well as sharpening public awareness of the poster, has also served to cloud its image. Initially, sales were geared to exploitation of classic reprints. Posters by Toulouse-Lautrec, Chéret, Mucha and a number of other artists formed the hard core. To these were added nostalgic or 'comic' turn-of-the-century items (posters for corsets, home exercisers and the like). Next came a wave of resurrected Aubrey Beardsley. (Beardsley, in fact, designed only a few posters, but he was now republished willy-nilly in poster form, book illustrations and all.)

Afterwards came World War I: *Your Country Needs You* and *I Want You For US Army*. Reprints of film and circus posters of the 1920s came soon after, and then, because ideas were running out, the poster reprint companies began to commission posters. These, original designs prepared especially for the market, were of two kinds: one was pop-psychedelia, the other was mock-commercial. In this second category posters were designed gratuitously for likely 'clients', sold to them for their own use on hoardings and simultaneously marketed in large numbers in poster shops. Thus, for example, collectors in New York found themselves b ying posters advertising London's Imperial War Museum—posters which, as it happened, had never seen action on the public hoardings.

The artificial generating of posters, coupled with indiscriminate posterisation of non-posters, led to confusion as to what a poster really is. Big photographic enlargements of pop stars, footballers and other celebrities joined the 'poster' stocks. So did pictures taken by astronauts, and so did photo nudes and sunsets and fields of waving corn. By the late 1960s the word 'poster' was being applied to any single visual presentation printed on a fair-sized sheet of paper. It was the age of the pseudo-poster.

The poster scene became progressively broader, more involuted, and in some sectors more costly. Typical of the trend was the case of an American pop-art poster exhibition, mounted in Sweden and publicised by a poster—the poster itself being subsequently exhibited in London (framed) for sale at some £25 sterling.

The poster, difficult to define precisely at the best of times, has today developed new areas of confusion. On present showing, these are likely to increase. The multiple influences that have worked on it in the past are themselves the subject of change. Television, the reprographic revolution, protest, pop and the rest—these are themselves in daily flux.

As with virtually every other aspect of life, in this latter part of the twentieth century there has been a sudden discontinuity. Instead of the logical progression that foresight might have looked for, there is a hiatus; an apparent break in the thread of evolution.

The poster, as it has been understood for three-quarters of a century, is unlikely to survive. It has grown up with the growth of the printing processes, adapting and improving with each stage of progress in the art. From a hazy concept, born on the one hand of the official notice and, on the other, of the trade announcement, it has fashioned for itself a specific identity, narrowed and refined its function, concentrated its power. At some time during the '20s or '30s (or was it the '50s?) it reached its zenith. At some time later (the '60s?), when printing began to spread to the office desk and the living-room table, the poster did so, too.

In 1970, on its last page, the book *Posters of Protest and Revolution* carried this paragraph:

> The Poster has passed through a number of clearly discernible historical stages. It has served variously as *vox Dei, vox populi* and *vox domini*; it has served as weapon of war, of commerce, of disaffection, irreverence, and seduction. It has been by turns a nuisance, a necessity, a menace—and, in the era of commercial TV, a premature bygone. As it settled down in the late '60s to being a cult object, suddenly it became everybody's protest standby. In the 1970s there are signs that the Poster may be starting a second time round.

Some eighteen months later, as this book goes to press, there are signs that, if the poster is indeed starting a second time round, it is doing so in a form so different as to be unrecognisable.

40

If it plese ony man spirituel or temporel to bye ony [co]pyes of two and three comemoracios of Salisbury use, emprynted after the forme of this present lettre whiche ben wel and truly correct, late hym come to Westmonester in the almonesrye at the reed pale and he shal have them good chepe. Supplico stet cedula [Please leave this paper]

Jf it plese ony man spirituel or temporel to bye ony pÿes of two and thre comemoracios of salisburi vse enpryntid after the forme of this preset lettre whiche ben wel and truly correct, late hym come to westmonester in to the almonestrye at the reed pale and he shal haue them good chepe.

Supplico stet cedula

1 BRITAIN 1477
William Caxton

Those who would distinguish them-selves in the service of the King in a fine Regiment may address themselves to Sieur Vaz de Mello, Cavalry Sergeant of the said Regiment who will offer them good enlistments . . . Those who bring good men will be rewarded.

2 FRANCE 1757
Anonymous

Herr Chiariny announces that today Dicke Maggarini will be in attendance with his Great Leaps. He will (1) leap in a somersault over 20 men, (2) leap over six horses, each mounted with its rider, (3) leap through a great barrel 20 feet in the air, which is a great and very dangerous leap. After these feats there follow the Great Equestrian Feats etc, etc . . . never before seen in Germany.

3 GERMANY
c 1770
Anonymous

DRAGONS
DE MONSEIGNEUR LE DUC D'ORLEANS.
PREMIER PRINCE DU SANG.

DE PAR LE ROI

CEUX qui voudront se distinguer au Service du Roi, dans un beau Régiment, peuvent s'adresser au Sieur VAZ DE MELLO, Maréchal-des-Logis audit Régiment, qui leur donnera de bons Engagemens.
Il loge rue Barbatre, chez Madame la veuve Blondeau, à Reims.
On peut aussi s'adresser à M. HEDOUIN DE PONSLUDON, Volontaire audit Régiment, rue de la grosse Clef. 1757
On a besoin d'un Freter, d'un Maréchal & d'un Sellier. On récompensera ceux qui amèneront de beaux hommes.

Mit gnädiger Erlaubniß einer hohen Obrigkeit
macht
Herr Chiariny

bekannt, daß heute der dicke Maggarini mit seinen grossen Luftspringen seine Aufwartung machen wird. Er wird 1) über 20 Mann durch einen Salto mortale in der Luft über sie springen. 2) Wird er über 6 Pferde worauf die Reuter sitzen über sie hinüber springen. 3) Wird er durch ein grosses zugemachtes Faß 20 Schuh von der Erde erhöht durch einen Salto mortale durchspringen, welches ein grosser und sehr gefährlicher Sprung ist. Nach diesen grossen Luftsprüngen folgen die grossen Reitkunsten. Es werden 1) die Herren Mayländer sich durch ihr geschicktes Voltigiren auf verschiedene Art auszeichnen. 2) Wird Mademoiselle Chiariny heute durch einen Hut über 6 Bänder vor und rückwärts springen. 3) Wird von einem Pferd und Reuter darauf der grosse Faßsprung in grossem Galopp wiederholt werden. Zum Beschluß wird Herr Chiariny den wilden Tiger, welcher dieser Tagen über 1 und 2 Pferde gesprungen, ihn heute aber über 3 Pferde springen lassen. Dieser grosse Sprung ist gewiß noch nie in Deutschland gesehen worden; daher hoffet Herr Chiariny einen zahlreichen Zuspruch und wird wegen seines kurzen Aufenthalts allen möglichen Fleiß anwenden, das Publikum auf das Beste zu unterhalten.

Der Schauplatz ist in dem hiesigen Fechthause.

Die Preise der Plätze sind:
Auf dem ersten Platz 36 kr. Auf dem zweyten 24 kr. Auf dem dritten 12 kr. und auf dem letzen Platz 6 kr.

Der Anfang ist Punkt halb vier Uhr.
Die Cassa wird um halb drey Uhr eröfnet.

4 ITALY 1799
Anonymous

AVVISO

Per ordine del Comandante Militare Austriaco di questa Città viene intimato a tutti gl'Abitanti in essa, di denunciare per iscritto al Maggiore della Piazza, che abita in Casa Mareschlchi, entro questo stesso giorno tutti gl'Individui Francesi, siano Uo-mini, che Donne, che albergano nelle proprie loro abitazioni, denunziando ancora tutti gl'effetti, che ad essi Individui appartengono. Si faccia ciascuno un dovere di ubbidire al presente ordine, altrimenti cadrà nelle pene Militari che gli verranno inflitte dal suddetto Comandante.
Bologna questo di 1. Luglio 1799.

Il Barone di KIRCHBERG
Maggiore della Piazza

By Order of the Austrian Military Command of the City, inhabitants are in-formed that they must declare in writing to the Maggiore within 24 hours, the names of all French people, men or women, living in their own homes, declaring also all property and effects belonging to them. It is incumbent upon all to obey this order, otherwise they will be subject to military punish-ments imposed by the undersigned Commander

—Kirchberg, Maggiore.

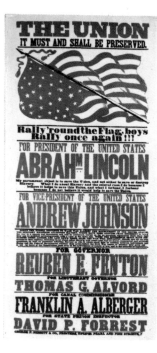

43

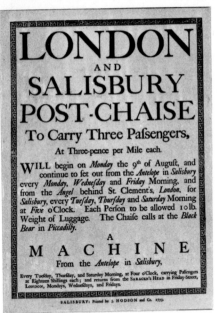

8 BRITAIN 1773
Anonymous

9 FRANCE c 1840
Anonymous

Military Replacements: Youths or veterans who would wish to take up service as replacements or substitutes in the French Army may apply, for the negotiating of contracts to Messrs Varnet & Co...Lyons. NB: Persons procuring replacements will be rewarded for their pains.

10 GERMANY c 1750
Anonymous

This is to announce that he who has a mind to it and would like to join the Infantry Regiment of the Distinguished Duke of Zerbst and serve therein, is invited to present himself at the recruiting centres in any of the towns of Augsburg, Oettingen, Memmingen and Schwäbisch-Hall. NB: He will receive a bounty as well as the measure of beer.

11 BRITAIN 1781
Anonymous

First Battalion of PENNSYLVANIA LOYALISTS,
commanded by His Excellency Sir WILLIAM
HOWE, K.B.

ALL INTREPID ABLE-BODIED

HEROES,

WHO are willing to serve His MAJESTY KING
GEORGE the Third, in Defence of their
Country, Laws and Constitution, against the arbitrary
Usurpations of a tyrannical Congress, have now not
only an Opportunity of manifesting their Spirit, by
assisting in reducing to Obedience their too-long de-
luded Countrymen, but also of acquiring the polite
Accomplishments of a Soldier, by serving only two
Years, or during the present Rebellion in America.

Such spirited Fellows, who are willing to engage,
will be rewarded at the End of the War, besides their
Laurels, with 50 Acres of Land, where every gallant
Hero may retire, and enjoy his Bottle and Lass.

Each Volunteer will receive, as a Bounty, FIVE
DOLLARS, besides Arms, Cloathing and Accoutre-
ments, and every other Requisite proper to accommo-
date a Gentleman Soldier, by applying to Lieutenant
Colonel ALLEN, or at Captain KEARNY's Ren-
dezvous, at PATRICK TONRY's, three Doors above
Market-street, in Second-street.

12 AMERICA c 1776
Anonymous

Se. Majestät haben die Errichtung einer Nationalgarde zur
Aufrechthaltung der gesetzmäßigen Ruhe und Ordnung der
Residenz und zum Schutze der Personen und des Eigenthumes,
und zwar unter den Garantien, welche sowohl den Besitz als die
Intelligenz dem Staate darbieten zu bewilligen geruht, und
versehen Sich von der Treue und der Ergebenheit Ihrer Unter-
thanen, daß Sie dem Ihnen bewiesenen Vertrauen entsprechen
werden.

Zugleich haben Se. Majestät Ihren Oberstjägermeister und
Feldmarschall-Lieutenant Grafen von Hoyos zum Befehls-
haber der Nationalgarde ernannt.

Wien am 14. März 1848.

Johann Talatzko Freih. von Gestieticz,
k. k. Nieder-Oester. Regierungs-Präsident.

**13 AUSTRIA-
HUNGARY** 1848
Anonymous

*His Majesty has graciously permitted the setting up of a National
Guard for the purpose of maintaining Law and Order in the Royal.
Precinct and for the protection of the person and of property …
and expects from his loyal subjects that they will live up to the
confidence reposed in them. At the same time he has appointed
Field Marshal Lieutenant Count von Hohos, Chief of the Hunt,
as Commander of the National Guard.*

*Vienna, March 14 1848
—Johann von Gestieticz*

TO BE SOLD & LET

BY PUBLIC AUCTION,
On MONDAY the 18th of MAY. 1829,
UNDER THE TREES.
FOR SALE,

THE THREE FOLLOWING

SLAVES,

VIZ.
HANNIBAL, about 30 Years old, an excellent House Servant, of Good Character.
WILLIAM, about 35 Years old, a Labourer.
NANCY, an excellent House Servant and Nurse.
The MEN belonging to "LEECH'S" Estate, and the WOMAN to Mrs. D. SMIT

TO BE LET,

On the usual conditions of the Hirer finding them in Food, Cloth in'c and Medical   ance,
THE FOLLOWING

MALE and FEMALE

SLAVES,

OF GOOD CHARACTERS,
ROBERT BAGLEY, about 20 Years old, a good House Servant.
WILLIAM BAGLEY, about 18 Years old, a Labourer.
JOHN ARMS, about 18 Years old.
JACK ANTONIA, about 40 Years old, a Labourer.
PHILIP, an Excellent Fisherman.
HARRY, about 27 Years old, a good House Servant.
LUCY, a Young Woman of good Character, used to House Work and the Nursery.
ELIZA, an Excellent Washerwoman.
CLARA, an Excellent Washerwoman.
FANNY, about 14 Years old, House Servant.
SARAH, about 14 Years old, House Servant.

Also for Sale, at Eleven o'Clock,

Fine Rice, Gram, Paddy, Books, Muslins, Needles, Pins, Ribbons, &c. &c.

AT ONE O'CLOCK, THAT CELEBRATED ENGLISH HORSE

BLUCHER,

ADDISON PRINTER GOVERNMENT OFFICE.

VENTE

DE
MEUBLES ET EFFETS
DE LA CI-DEVANT REINE,
PROVENANT DU PETIT TRIANON,
EN VERTU DE LA LOI DU DIX JUIN DERNIER.

Le Dimanche 13 Août 1791, l'on deuxième de la République une & indivisible, 10 heures du matin, & 4 heures de relevée, & jours suivans.

SAVOIR:

Tous les maines, BAterie & ustensiles de cuisine & d'office, ferrailles & meubles communs.
Tous les soirs Meubles de luxe, consistans en Lits avec leurs housses de différentes étoffes, armoires, secrétaires, commodes, tables, credities, parties à dessus de marbre, sieux, chaises longues, fauteuils, canapés, banquettes, chaises à tabourets de damas, lampas, velours de soie d'Utrecht, & moquette, sauence, vannerie, porcelaine d'office & de table.

Les neufs Meubles de toute espèce, & en grande quantité, seront annoncés par de nouvelles affiches.

Ceux venir si sera en présence des Représentans du Peuple, & des Commissaires du District, au ci-devant Château de Versailles.

N.B. Les Meubles de la ci-devant Liste civile peuvent être transportés à l'étranger, en exemption de tous droits.

Les Commissaires de la Convention Nationale.
CH. DELACROIX, J.M. MUSSET.

15 FRANCE 1791
Anonymous

*Sale of furniture and effects of the former
Queen, from the Petit Trianon, by virtue
of the Law of June 10 last. Each morning:
kitchen and pantry gear and utensils etc,
etc... each evening: domestic furniture
etc, etc...*

14 AMERICA 1829
Anonymous

16 ITALY 1859
Anonymous

Notice: All public officials are ordered to remain at their posts and to proceed without delay upon the discharge of their duties, except for any special instructions the Government may give.— on behalf of General Garibaldi: Emilio Visconti Venosta

AVVISO

Bergamo, li 8 Giugno 1859.

Si ordina a tutti i pubblici funzionarj di rimanere ai loro posti e di attendere senza ritardo al disimpegno delle loro mansioni, salvo quelle particolari disposizioni che il Governo credesse di prendere.

IL REGIO COMMISSARIO STRAORDINARIO PRESSO IL
GENERALE GARIBALDI
EMILIO VISCONTI VENOSTA.

Bergamo : della Tipografia Pagnoncelli.

DÉPARTEMENT DE POLICE.

La négligence de quelques citoyens, sur la propreté des rues, force de rappeler à tous et un chacun les mesures anciennement prescrites, qui doivent continuer d'être observées. En conséquence il est enjoint à tous les citoyens, et ce sous les peines portées par l'Art. XV du Titre I. de la Loi sur la Police municipale, de faire balayer exactement devant leurs maisons, de manière que les rues soient nettoyées, savoir à six heures du matin du premier avril au premier octobre, et à sept heures du matin du premier octobre au premier avril. Il est également défendu de ne point porter ou faire porter des immondices ou balayures aux coins des rues après sept heures du matin en été, et après huit heures en hiver. Il est ordonné à l'entrepreneur de faire enlever les balayures, boues et immondices, savoir dans la ville jusqu'à onze heures du matin, et dans les fauxbourgs, conformément à l'ancien usage. Les Commissaires de police tiendront la main aux réglemens sur la propreté des rues; et il est ordonné aux gardes de police de faire exactement leurs tournées, et de dénoncer les contrevenans.

Fait à Strasbourg le 14 Novembre 1791.

Signé: Dietrich, *Maire.*

Pasquay,
Administrateur de la police.

Par ordonnance,
Guérin,
Secrétaire en chef.

Polizey-Verwaltung.

Die Nachläßigkeit in der Säuberung der Straßen, nöthigt die Verwaltung alle Bürger an die alten Verordnungen zu erinnern, welche darüber vorhanden und immerfort beobachtet werden sollen. Diesemnach ist es allen Bürgern anbefohlen, und zwar bei der Strafe, die im 15 Artikel des ersten Titels vom Munizipal-Polizei-Gesetz vorgeschrieben ist, vor ihren Häusern ordnungsmäßig fegen zu lassen, so daß die Straßen gesäubert seyn sollen, nemlich um sechs Uhr Morgens vom ersten April bis den ersten Oktober, und um sieben Uhr Morgens vom ersten Oktober bis den ersten April. Es ist auch jedermänniglich verboten, irgend einen Unrath oder Auskehricht nach sieben Uhr Morgens im Sommer, und nach acht Uhr im Winter auf die Straßen oder an deren Ecken zu tragen. Dem Unternehmer der Straßen-Säuberung ist es anbefohlen, den Auskehricht, Unrath und Koth fortführen zu lassen, und zwar in der Stadt bis eilf Uhr Morgens, und in den Vorstädten, wie es bisher gebräuchlich war. Die Polizei-Kommissarien sollen ein wachsames Aug auf die Vollziehung der Verordnungen über die Reinigung der Straßen haben, und den Polizei-Garden ist es anbefohlen, ihre vorgeschriebene Besuche der Straßen auf das genaueste vorzunehmen, und die Uebertreter der Verordnungen anzuzeigen.

Gegeben zu Straßburg den 14 November 1791.
Unterschrieben Dietrich, Maire.
Pasquay, Polizei-Verwalter.
Auf Befehl,
Guerin,
Ober-Sekretär.

Gedruckt bey Ph. J. Dannbach, der Munizipalität Buchdrucker.

---

18 USA c 1865
Anonymous

WILL BE EXHIBITED
FOR ONE DAY ONLY!
AT THE STOCKTON HOUSE!
THIS DAY, AUG. 19, FROM 9 A. M. UNTIL 6 P. M.
THE HEAD
Of the renowned Bandit!
JOAQUIN!
AND THE
HAND OF THREE FINGERED JACK!
THE NOTORIOUS ROBBER AND MURDERER.

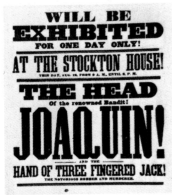

---

19 FRANCE 1840 Anonymous

DÉCRET

Le PRINCE NAPOLÉON au nom du PEUPLE FRANÇAIS décrète ce qui suit:
La Dynastie des Bourbons d'Orléans a cessé de régner.
Le Peuple Français est rentré dans ses droits.
Les Troupes sont déliées du serment de Fidélité.
La Chambre des Pairs et la Chambre des Députés sont dissoutes. Un congrès national sera convoqué dès l'arrivée du Prince Napoléon à Paris.
Monsieur Thiers Président du Conseil est nommé à Paris Président du Gouvernement Provisoire.
Le Maréchal Clausel est nommé Commandant en chef des Troupes rassemblées à Paris.
Le Général Pajol conserve le commandement de la première Division Militaire.
Tous les Chefs de corps qui ne se conformeront pas sur le champ ces ordres seront remplacés.
Tous les Officiers, sous-Officiers et Soldats qui montreront énergiquement leur sympathie pour la cause nationale, seront récompensés d'une manière éclatante au nom de la Patrie.
Dieu protège la France!

signé: **NAPOLÉON**

Boulogne le   1840

Decree: The Prince Napoleon in the name of the French People, decrees as follows: The dynasty of the Bourbons d'Orleans has ceased to reign; the French People are reinstated in their rights: the troops are absolved from their oaths of allegiance; both Chambers are dissolved. A National Congress will be called on the arrival of Prince Napoleon in Paris. . . Commanders who fail to conform immediately to these orders are hereby replaced. God protect France!

partment of Police: The negligence of
ain citizens in the matter of street
nliness obliges the drawing of atten-
of one and all to the measure lately
orce and whose observance must
tinue. Accordingly, all citizens are
ained . . . carefully to sweep in front
heir houses, so that the streets be
ned . . . The contractor is instructed
emove sweepings in the town until
en o'clock in the morning and in the
skirts according to earlier usage. . . .

HIGHGATE
CADET CORPS.

The Uniform for this Corps (which is now in course of formation),
received the unanimous approval of the

14th MIDDLESEX
(HIGHGATE)

RIFLE VOLUNTEERS,

When introduced to that distinguished Corps by

MAJOR WILKINSON,

On the 22nd of June.

It may be seen, and full particulars obtained of

G. BRAYSHAW,
TAILOR,

No. 4, MORETON TERRACE,

Between the Hawley and Clarence Roads,

KENTISH TOWN.

This Uniform is generally pronounced to be the smartest and most
becoming for a Cadet Corps hitherto brought out, and possesses
the great advantage of being readily converted into a neat private
dress.

Young Gentlemen wishing to join, can give their names to
Sergeant-Major PRATT, Head Quarters, Southwood Lane, Highgate, or to G. BRAYSHAW, as above.

Cost of Uniform complete - £1 18s.

Drill Ground for Kentish Town,
NATIONAL SCHOOLS, ISLIP STREET.

Uniform for the Highgate Rifle Volunteers - - £4 15s.

20   BRITAIN   c 1880   Anonymous

THE WOMAN IN WHITE

OLYMPIC THEATRE

21   BRITAIN   1871
Frederick Walker RA
(Engraved by W. H. Hooper)

COLORED
ENGRAVINGS
FOR THE
PEOPLE
PUBLISHED BY
N. CURRIER
LITHOGRAPHER,
2 Spruce Street
NEW-YORK.
FOR SALE HERE.

22   USA   c 1880
Anonymous

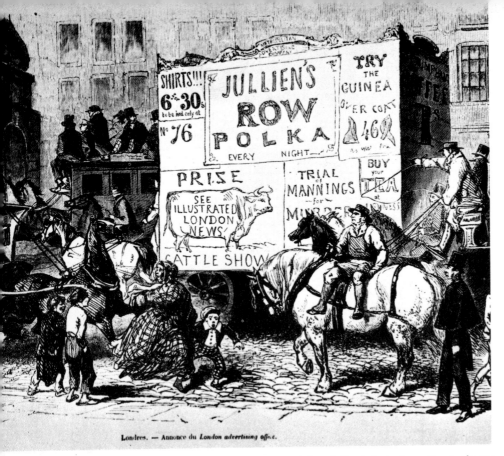

London in the 1850s: early billposting contractors moved from indiscriminate fly-posting to the use of 'advertising carts'—mobile hoardings which tangled the traffic of the town. It was at this period that London contractors, seeking respectability, began calling themselves 'external paper-hangers'.

Paris, 1840: France's first attempt to tame the poster was the 'publicity column'—still widely used in the '70s.

In Italy the poster was a late starter. It was identified in the public mind specifically with war and unrest. This batch is part of the output for 1848.

As billposting became mor orderly (top picture), anarch gave way to organised deface

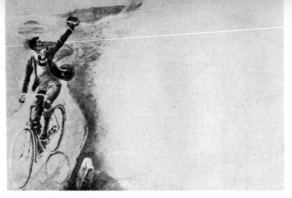

The general-purpose poster: designed for use by any number of different bicycle manufacturers, this 1890s design leaves space for overprinting of the advertiser's name and message.

This Russian poster footnote (1919) threatens punishment for defacement.

Turn-of-the-century magazines—one for the bill poster, another for the connoisseur—reflect the rising influence of the medium. The international collector's list on the right, published in Germany's magazine Das Plakat, *shows current market prices for poster specimens.*

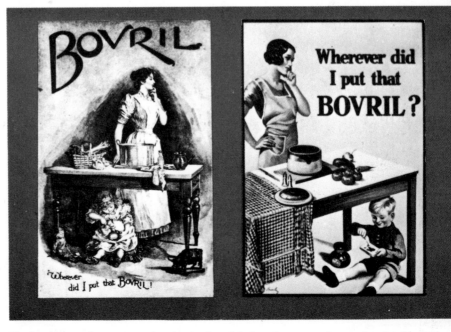

The late nineteenth century produced a number of designs that were to become imprinted on the folk-memory. The poster on the left appeared in 1899 and aroused attention amounting almost to the point of affection. Up-dated in 1937 however, it went virtually un-noticed.

ent. Contractors rented their n permanent sites and prided emselves on a smart turn-out.

NB Names of countries appearing in captions refer throughout to place of publication, not necessarily to nationality of the artist.

24 BRITAIN 1896
Sir John Millais

23 ITALY c 1901
Luigi Bompard
Venice Journal

25 FRANCE 1898
F. Vallotton
Edouard Sagot, Print and Poster Dealer

30   FRANCE   1896
Jean Paléologue

FRANCE   1894
Chéret
...alace, Champs Elysées

28   ITALY   1899
Adolfo Hohenstein
Calliano Sea-sick Belt

31   FRANCE   c 1900
F. Lunel

29   ITALY   c 1900
Aleardo Villa
'Caffaro': Fashion Journal

32   FRANCE   1899
Théophile Steinlen
Comiot Motor cycles

33   ITALY   1900
Anonymous

35   BRITAIN   1894
Théophile Steinlen

34   FRANCE   1894
Alfons Mucha

'*Gismonda*': *Sarah Bernhardt at the*
Théâtre Renaissance

37 USA 1895
William H. Bradley

40 FRANCE 189[
Alfons Muc[

'Job' Cigarette Pape[

36 BRITAIN c 1894
Aubrey Beardsley

38 FRANCE 1894
Théophile Steinlen

*Exhibition of the Works
of T. A. Steinlen*

39 GERMANY 1896
Otto Fischer

'The Old Town': Exhibition of
Saxon Arts and Crafts

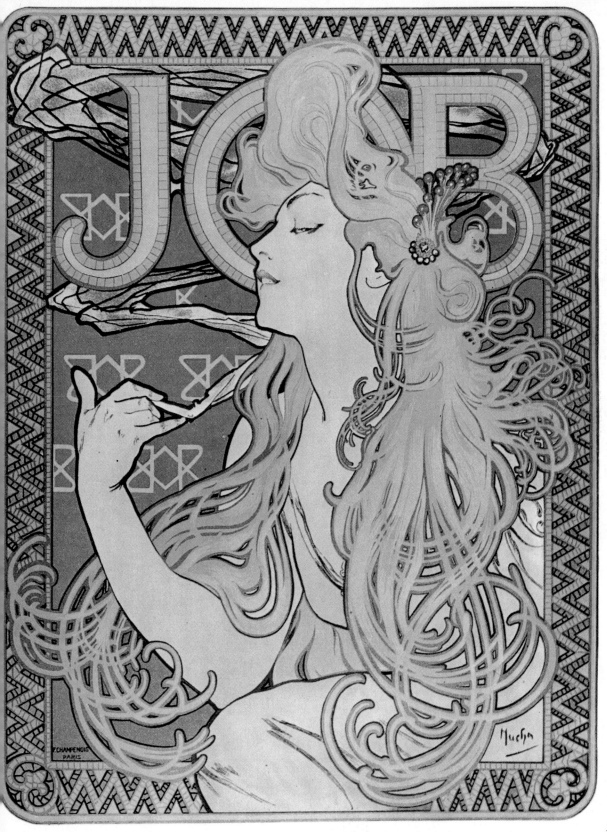

57

41 ITALY 1908
Leopoldo M. Metlicovitz

('Mele': a famous fashion store)

42   FRANCE c 1895
E. Dorda

43   BRITAIN c 1902
B. H. Smale

44 BRITAIN 1900
Beggarstaff Brothers
(James Pryde and
William Nicholson)

45 ITALY c 1900
Adolfo Hohenstein
'*Italia*' Beer

The billboard took a long time to settle down. The Paris publicity ladies (1900) were partly an advertising novelty and partly an answer to increasingly rigorous fly-posting laws. In the United States (right) the outsize poster came in at an early stage and was to remain the basic American outdoor publicity unit for half a century. This one, 'the first-ever for Ansco', appeared in 1919.

Many early posters, conceived on the assumption that they would be appropriate for any one of a number of possible advertisers, were designed speculatively. Without briefing or instruction, artists carried out finished work and hawked it round to potential clients. The advertiser's name was inserted on acceptance. This oil-painting, complete with notional brand-name, failed to find a buyer.

By the turn of the century the poster artist had achieved full celebrity status. Dudley Hardy (left), here posing before his latest work, expresses the mood exactly. More positive, and with a more conscious eye to the invited press photographers, James Montgomery Flagg stages a mock re-paint of his US Marines poster on the forecourt outside the New York Public library.

The new century saw the beginning of the widespread use of posters in political propaganda. In Soviet Russia the poster was very soon established as a major medium. The picture shows a propaganda train fitted out as a mobile exhibition and with carriage sides treated as panoramic posters. In the picture on the right, Italy's first post-war election posters are being pasted up.

Posters were used in safety propaganda from an early date. In the picture, taken shortly after World War I, a lithographic pictorial poster warns civilians of the dangers of touching battlefield debris.

Plagiarism, 1906: apart from details of the bow, the drawin of the shoe are mirror-image twins. Which of these poste appeared first is unrecorded. Artists were F. H. Warre

France, 1916: 'The End of the War in 60–80 Days'. The means to an early victory were destined never to be revealed. The poster, seized by the censor's office before completion, was not published.

Plagiarism was a long-standing grievance in the advertising world. Even in the stress of war a German magazine found tim for 'exposées'. The illustrations show (left and centre) th

By the 1890s the poster had become a French cultural
institution—itself the subject of publicity. This one,
advertising a big printer, was a poster for posters.

49 FRANCE   1896
Théophile Steinlen

Charles Verneau: Posters

reat Britain; Lucian Bernhard, Germany.
any such examples remained undiscover-
d till chance comparison in poster archives.

50   FRANCE   c 1898
Alfred Choubrac

'Fin de Siècle':
Illustrated Literary Journal

leged ingredients of the 'Kämpft mit'
ar-loan poster. The silhouette, added to
e flame background, gives a new poster.

Choubrac often fell foul of the censor. On this occasion he erased part of the drawing
and added the gratuitous wording 'This Part of the Design has been Forbidden'. Not
surprisingly the amendment attracted even more attention than the original.

51 GERMANY 1911
Hans Rudi Erdt

54 ITALY c
Aleardo T
'Novissi
Annual of

52 USA c 1900
William H. Bradley

'53 USA 1907
Louis Fancher

55   USA   c 1900
Anonymous

56   GERMANY   1914
Anonymous

The prosecution of war operations obliges me to move my Headquarters away from Berlin. I speak from the bottom of my heart when I bid farewell to the citizens of Berlin and thank them for the demonstrations of love and affection which I have experienced in so rich a measure in these great and fateful days. I have supreme confidence in the help of God, in the bravery of the Army and the Navy and in the unbreakable sense of unity of the German people in their hour of peril. Victory will not fail a just cause.

Berlin, August 16 1914
—Wilhelm IR

AMERICANS ALL!
HONOR ROLL
Du Bois
Smith
O'Brien
Cejka
Haucke
Pappandrikopolous
Andrassi
Villotto
Levy
Turovich
Kowalski
Chriczanevicz
Knutson
Gonzales
Howard Chandler Christy 1919

9   USA   1917
ames Montgomery Flagg

60   FRANCE   1918
'Sem'

For the last quarter of an hour—help me!
Subscriptions to the National Loan:
received at the National Credit Bank

61   BRITAIN   1915
Alfred Leete

62   GERMANY   1918
Ludwig Hohlwein

Exhibition of Work by German
Internees in Switzerland

RICHTER & Cº
NAPOLI

"FINALMENTE!"

VIª
PRESTITO
NAZIONALE

63 ITALY
1918
Mario Borgoni
'At last!':
National Loan

66 BRITAIN c 1922
'RAE'

PEACE

The Evening News

65 BRITAIN 1919
Anonymous

THE BLUES

POPULAR CAFÉ

IT WILL COST YOU NOTHING
TO DANCE THEM AWAY AT THE

VISITORS TAKING DINNER SUPPER OR
TEA MAY DANCE AT NO EXTRA CHARGE

allez chez
Poccard

Son Restaurant : 9, Bᵈ des Itali
Son Restaurant : 12, Rue Favar
Son Bar : 34, Rue Sᵗ Marc
PARIS

ADOLPH WILUTZKY
KÖNIGSBERG I. PR.

EUE HAUS DER TECHNIK IN
KÖNIGSBERG I.PR.,
NWEIHUNG ZUR ELFTEN DEUTSCHEN
STMESSE AM 16. AUGUST 1925.

68
GERMANY
1924
(...?)

FRANCE

etto
piello

FRÜHLING

69 GERMANY
c 1928
Ludwig Hohlwein
*Spring in
Wiesbaden*

IN WIESBADEN

73   BRITAIN
1924
John Hassall

71   FRANCE   1927
Leonetto Cappiello

*'Sizaire': Suspension and
Steering make it Independent
of the Road*

72   BRITAIN   1927
Gregory Brown

74   USA   c 1920
Anonymous

GERMANY   1927
pp Wiertz

75 BRITAIN   1928
Frank Newbould

77 ITALY   1927
Leopoldo M. Metlicovitz
*'Cidam': A non-profit-
making concern*

76 GERMANY   1922
Fritz Koch Gotha
'The Week': Don't Forget!

78 USSR   c 1927
Anonymous
*Money gone? But what
about the family?*

81 BRITAIN 1927
Tom Purvis

82 ITALY 1928
Lucio Venna
Viareggio Carnival

83 BRITAIN 1925
F. Gardner

84 USA c 1926
Anonymous

85 FRANCE 1926
René Vincent

86 USA c 1926
Anonymous

87 GERMANY 1926
Hans Rosen
To Berlin!

88 ITALY 1927
—Santambrogio
San Giorgio:
Electro-mechanical
constructions

JEDER EINMAL IN
BERLIN

NACH
BERLIN!

Auskunft erteilen die Reise- und Verkehrsbüros, sowie das Ausstellungs-, Messe- und Fremdenverkehrs-Amt der Stadt Berlin

SAN GIORGIO
GENOVA - SESTRI

OSTRUZIONI-ELETTROMECCANICHE

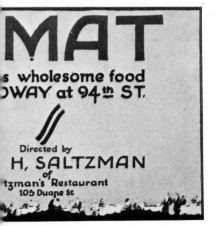

MAT
s wholesome food
OWAY at 94th ST.

Directed by
H. SALTZMAN
of
tzman's Restaurant
105 Duane St

"SHELL"

89 BRITAIN
c 1926
Charles Fouqueray

78

95   GERMANY   1918
Alfred Stiller
'The Red Flag' (Journal)

96   ITALY   1926
Marcello Dudovich
'La Rinascente' (Fashion Store)

97   BRITAIN   1927   Dora Batty

Don't miss Autumn's Splendours

94   USSR   1930
D. S. Moor
(Dimitri Stakheyevitch Orlov)

Proletarians, be on your guard!
The 'Black Crows' [The Priests] are
preparing an attack on the USSR

98   FRANCE   1927
A. Mouron Cassandre
'North Star' Pullman Service

          (Right)
99   BRITAIN   1927
Horace Taylor

100　BRITAIN　1927
A. Mouron Cassandre

101　SWITZERLAND　c 1926
Marcello Nizzoli

102　BRITAIN　1926
Tom Purvis

The relief printing principle: pictures show (left) early hand-carved wooden characters (for cheap poster work still in widespread use in the 1970s) and a modern printer's 'forme' containing metal type and half-tone printing block. Relief printing is rarely used in large-scale commercial poster production.

No longer in general use for posters, the lithographic stone carried a water-repellent greasy image (top left) and accepted roller ink (lower picture) only in image areas. Pressed into contact with paper, the inked image was 'lifted' from the stone (right). Repeated inking allowed multiple printings.

today's photo-lithography the image is applied photographically
sheets of zinc. 4-colour negatives are prepared electronically (top
cture); plates are wrapped round printing rollers (lower picture).

ОКНО ТАСС № 113
РА-КО ДНУ!

duced for indoor use, some Russian World War II posters
nbined hand-stencilling with wood-block printing. First picture
ws complete poster; second and third show paste-up details.

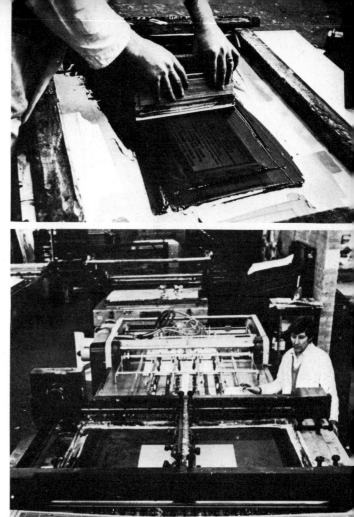

In silk-screen printing (top picture) ink is squeegeed on to paper
through a fine-mesh stencil. Today's machines (lower picture) have
transformed a hand operation into a high-speed precision process. 83

84

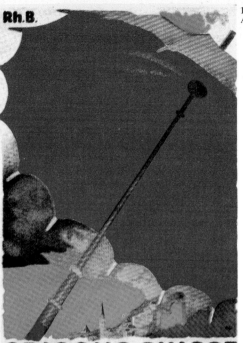

104   SWITZERLAND   1927
Augusto Giacometti

105   USSR   1931
Anonymous

In 1931 Let us Provide Eight Million Tons of Cast-Iron for the Construction of Socialism

106   SWITZERLAND   1931
Ernst Keller

Walter Gropius Exhibition

107   BRITAIN
1936
Barnett Freedman

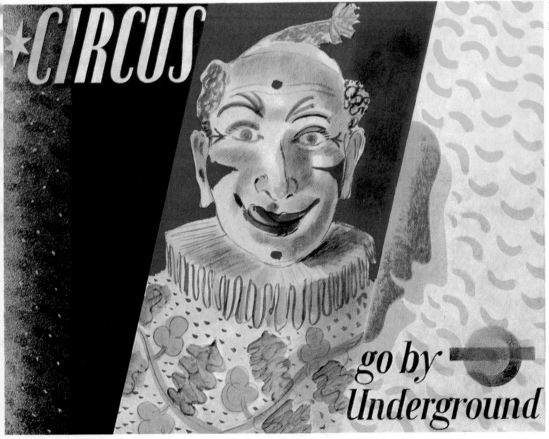

108 ITALY
c 1936
Anonymous
*Nord-Milan
Railways*

109 FRANCE
1932
Jean Carlu
For Disarmament

112 NORWAY 1935
Herbert Matter
Drive to Switzerland!

113 USSR 1931
Anonymous

*Into the Schools; Into the Factories;
Into Public Life!
Extend the network of day nurseries
and canteens; liberate millions of
women for participation in
Socialist reconstruction!*

DEUTSCHE KAUFT DEUTSCHE WARE

DEUTSCHE
WOCHE
DEUTSCHE
WARE
DEUTSCHE
ARBEIT

KEIMEL

114 GERMANY 1931
Hermann Keimel

German Week; German Goods; German Work!

115 ITALY 1931
Marcello Nizzoli
Milan Fair

(Right)
116 ITALY 1932
Marcello Dudovich
Fiat: the new Balilla for everyone; feminine elegance!

117 USA 1934
Anonymous

118 FRANCE 1932
A. Mouron Cassandre

120   BRITAIN
1936
E. McKnight
Kauffer

121 FRANCE 1930
Leonetto Cappiello
'Kub' soup cubes

124 GERMANY 19
Willy Petzo
Oberschlema Radium Bar
—Strongest in the Wor

122 GERMANY 1932
Ludwig Hohlwein
. . . AND YOU?

123 SPAIN c 1937
Anonymous
All Militias United in
the People's Army

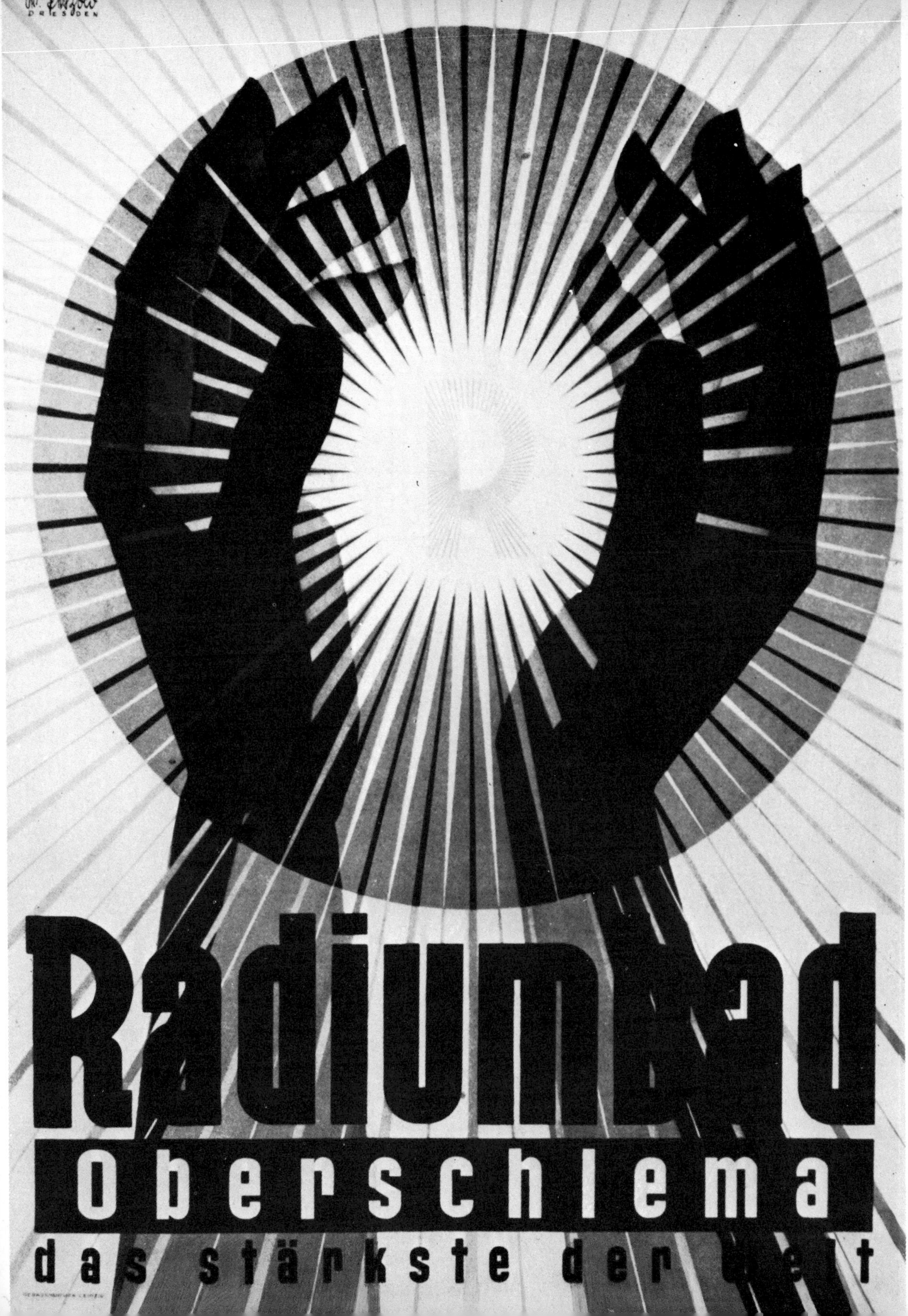

Radiumbad
Oberschlema
das stärkste der Welt

THE FAMOUS PARIS RESTAURANT

MAISON
PRUNIER

72 St. JAMES'S STREET
LONDON

Reichswettkampf der SA

126   GERMANY   c 1934
Elk Eber (?)
National Storm Troop Contest

128   FRANCE   1930
Francis Bernard
Visit Morocco

129   FRANCE   1937
Austin Cooper
Paris Fair

Air Raid Wardens
WANTED

AND THEY ARE WANTED
NOW
GET INTO TOUCH WITH YOUR LOCAL COUNCIL

Foire de PARIS

15·30 mai 1937

25   BRITAIN
·35
. Mouron Cassandre

127   BRITAIN
1939
C. W. Bacon

131 USA 1941
John Atherton

a careless word

...another cross

130 FRANCE c 1942
Anonymous

If you want France to live you will fight in the Waffen SS against Bolshevism

(In the second picture the caption has been amended by partial obliteration. It reads: *If you want France to live, you will fight against the Boche*)

132 USA 1941
Jean Carlu

133 GERMANY 1941
Ludwig Hohlwein
Air raid precautions

94

YOUR TALK
MAY KILL YOUR COMRADES

134   BRITAIN   1942
Abram Games

Soldati italiani!

La triste ora del tradimento e della vergogna è passata.

Tenete fede al vostro Duce!

Unitevi alle truppe germaniche che lo hanno liberato e con loro difendete la vostra Patria

contro i nemici del popolo italiano
contro i nemici dell' Europa!

Seguite l'esempio di tanti vostri commilitoni. Presentatevi al più vicino comando germanico.

Vi sarete accolti con grande cameratismo!

135   ITALY   1943 Anonymous

Italian Soldiers! The sad hour of treachery and shame is past. Have faith in your Leader! Join the German troops who have freed him; with them, defend your country—against the enemies of the Italian people— against the enemies of Europe! Follow the example of so many of your comrades in arms. Go to the nearest German unit. You will be received with friendliness

non tradite mio figlio

136   ITALY   1943   Gino Boccasile
Don't break faith with my son!

SOTTOSCRIVETE
SI ARRENDERANNO

137   ITALY   1942
Gino Boccasile
*Buy War Loan
—they're surrendering!*

fuori i tedeschi

138   ITALY   1943
Anonymous
Germans out!

141   BRITAIN   1959
Maurice Rickards

140   GERMANY   1949 Anonymous

142   SWITZERLAND   1944
Gérard Meidinger

Swiss Winter Aid

143   BRITAIN   195
Abram Game

murphy television

144   BRITAIN   1946
William Little

145   POLAND   1953
Witold Chmielewski
Mariners' Day

146   SWITZERLAND   c 1954
Herbert Leupin
Better drink Eptinger!

147   ITALY   1958
Giovanni Pintori

PICASSO

Un demi-siècle de Livres Illustrés

du 21 Décembre 1956 au 31 Janvier 1957

GALERIE H. MATARASSO

36 Boulevard Dubouchage . NICE

148   FRANCE   1956
Pablo Picasso
Half a Century of Illustrated Books

VINCE
SEMPRE LA LANA

149   SWITZERLAND   1954
Donald Brun
Wool always wins

150   POLAND   1952
Tadeusz Trepkowski
NO!

151   USA   c 1960
Walter H. Allner

Cuba's sugar crop campaign is supported by massive poster publicity: 'We will not let the rains set us back'; 'Sugar must be cut to the last cane—if need be, to the last drop of blood'. The Castro portrait bears the caption: 'Revolutionaries are never demoralized.'

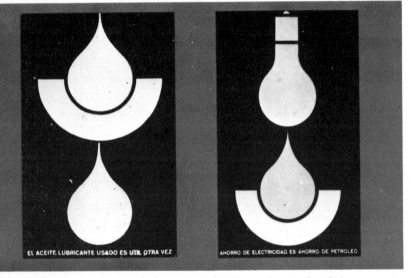

EL ACEITE LUBRICANTE USADO ES UTIL OTRA VEZ

AHORRO DE ELECTRICIDAD ES AHORRO DE PETROLEO

Stage-by-stage development of a poster idiom. The cup shape in the oil-economy poster (left) conveys 'saving'; in the second design the same shape is applied to electric-light economy. Felix Beltrán, Cuba's leading designer, has evolved a new 'visual grammar.'

The poster has played a major role in Cuba since the revolution. Huge poster portraits dominate the scene at mass outdoor rallies

In a spectacular campaign in France in the 1950s, the 'reminder' aspect of outdoor publicity was taken to a logical conclusion. Using only the shape and colour-scheme of the product name, the designer fragmented 'St Raphaël' to form an abstract but instantly recognisable pattern. On the left: an early stage of fragmentation; right: a typical end-state. The technique was also used on buses and delivery vans

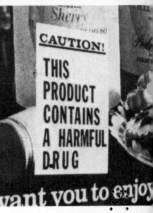

ADOLF
THAD
NPD

CAUTION!
THIS
PRODUCT
CONTAINS
A HARMFUL
DRUG
vant you to enjoy

Defacement flourishes: the semi-professional defacer has been the subject of at least one photo-journalist's report (left). In Paris (top right) warnings to defacers are themselves defaced (with pointed reference to the date of the decree). In Germany von Thadden's election poster is retouched, and in Britain a drink poster receives an unofficial over-sticker.

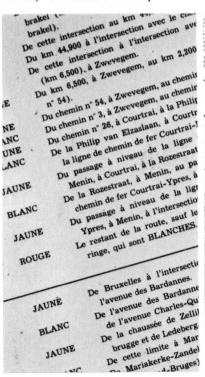

Civic and national authorities in most countries control the use of outdoor advertising, and national associations of bill-posting contractors collaborate in enforcing limitations. In Belgium a colour-coded national map classifies routes and localities in varying degrees of prohibition. In the photograph (right) areas of total prohibition appear as a grey tone. 101

With the spread of modern reprographic processes, the poster has become a voice for every shade of opinion. The poster shown here, photographed in Belfast, appeared in the windows of private houses during July 1970.

In 1971 the pop poster reached notable levels of illegibility; sideways fly-posting (top picture) was not uncommon; eccentric cut-outs also appeared.

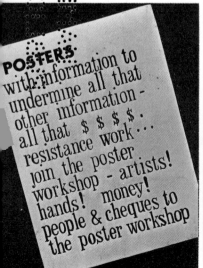

POSTERS with information to undermine all that other information – all that $ $ $ $. resistance work ... join the poster workshop – artists! hands! money! people & cheques to the poster workshop

The late '60s saw a burst of improvised graphics from protest groups in a number of countries. On the left is an announcement put out by one of a number of student 'information workshops', which produced a wide range of protest material on a co-operative basis; on the right is the scene in the poster workshop in Rome University after it had been vacated by occupying students.

The poster craze of the '60s and '70s became very big business. These poster catalogue sheets are a few of the many hundreds put out by publishers in a dozen countries. In the United States, aggregate annual turnover is computed at $3–$4 million. Many of the 'posters' are simple photo blow-ups; the word 'poster', now used for any large print, has begun to lose its identity.

This poster, advertising an exhibition of US pop and poster art in Sweden, was itself on display afterwards in a London decor showroom. Price: £22.50

Pseudo-posters of the 1970s: all these items, including 'London Zoo', were produced specifically for the poster-fad market. The World War I and II specimens are Imperial War Museum reproductions.

Paris, 1968: the design on the left, with lettering executed in reverse in error, was widely posted. It appeared in a corrected version (right) some time later.

152   ITALY   1960
Bruno Munari

154   BRITAIN   c 1965
Stan Krol

155   FRANCE   c 1953
Raymond Savignac
'Milk-soap'

也没有看见人民群众
样精神振奋，斗志昂
风发。 毛泽东

不胜的毛泽东思想万岁

parcels   very carefully

156   BRITAIN   c 1956
Tom Eckersley

FRONTIÈRES = REPRESSION

Long Live the Invincible Thoughts of Chairman Mao: The world has never before witnessed such enthusiasm, such combativeness, such proud confidence, among the masses. (Signed) Mao Tse Tung

157   FRANCE
1968
Anonymous
Frontiers mean repression

Fiera di Milano

14-25 aprile   1968

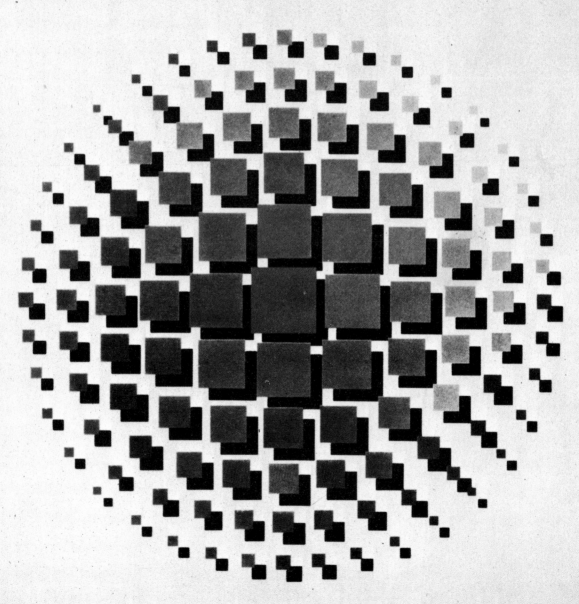

Centro Internazionale degli Scambi

158   ITALY   1968
Georg Erhardt/Ezio Bonini/Aldo Calabresi
Milan Fair

159   GERMANY   1964
Raymond Savignac
Cologne Carnival

160   CUBA   1968
Anonymous

161   USA   1964
Bob Hayman/Ed de Martin

162   USA   1964
Tomi Ungerer

Texaco. Rarin' to go.

TEXACO

163 BRITAIN 1971
Max Henry

Martell: Britain's favourite cognac since th

165 ITALY
1967
Carmelo Cremonesi
*Let's give a hand
to keep Milan tidy*

164 BRITAIN 1970 Richard Dearing / Adrian Flowers

.....aber meine Schutzbrille   trage ich immer

urn of the century.

Join the Tea-V set

166
SWITZERLAND
1966
Arthur Frei /
Heiner Grieder
'. . . but I always
wear my sunglasses'

167 BRITAIN
1970
Anonymous

168 USA
1968
Anonymous

169 BRITAIN 1969 Anonymous

170 ITALY 1970
Heinz Edelmann

171 USA 1971
Anonymous